A PATH TO LIBERATION

A Spiritual and Philosophical Approach to the Martial Arts

A PATH TO LIBERATION

A Spiritual and Philosophical Approach to the Martial Arts

HERMAN P. KAUZ

Photographs by Tetsu Okuhara
and Robert Reitter

THE OVERLOOK PRESS
Woodstock • New York

First published in 1992 by
The Overlook Press
Lewis Hollow Road
Woodstock, New York 12498

Library of Congress Cataloging-in-Publication Data

Kauz, Herman P.
    A path to liberation: a spiritual and philosophical approach to the
    martial arts/Herman P. Kauz; photographs by Tetsu Okuhara.
        p. cm.

    1. Martial arts — Philosophy. 2. Martial arts — psychological aspects.
    I. Title

GV1101.K39 1992
796.8—dc20

91-37524
CIP

ISBN 0-87951-423-X

All photographs by Tetsu Okuhara except pages vi, 78 and 100 by Robert Reitter.

10 9 8 7 6 5

CONTENTS

All photographs by Tetsu Okuhara except pages vi, 78 and 100 by Robert Reitter.

Acknowledgments

I AM GRATEFUL for the help given me over the years in my study and understanding of the martial arts by my teachers and students.

Thanks, also, to the director and staff of The Overlook Press who were kind enough to publish this book and to provide helpful editorial suggestions. Tom Funk deserves special mention for his sensitive editing.

My daughter, Emiko, patiently and almost uncomplainingly typed a number of versions of the manuscript.

The nature photographs of Bob Reitter and Tetsu Okuhara visually express the book's ideas. Tetsu captures the spirit of the various martial arts in his action shots. The work of Bob and Tetsu constitutes an invaluable contribution to the book's total effect.

The photographs that appear in this book were taken at the following schools: New York Aikikai, Y. Yamada, Chief Instructor; American Buddhist Academy Judo Club, N. Higashi, Judo Head Master; New York Karate Club, M. Mori, Chief Instructor; Japan Martial Arts Academy, Ken Zen Dojo, S. Kan, Chief Instructor; Midtown Tai Chi Club, H. Kauz, Instructor.

CHAPTER I

Introduction

> Households, cities, countries and nations
> have enjoyed great happiness when a single indi-
> vidual has taken heed of the Good and Beautiful
> .... Such men not only liberate themselves; they
> fill those they meet with a free mind.
>
> PHILO

MANY OF US who live in an urban setting in one of today's developed nations sense that we are living a large portion of our waking lives in a somewhat artificial environment. We experience the often depressing effect of the paved-over earth, buildings that surround us and shut out all but a small patch of sky, stressful days devoid of physical exercise, conditioned air, piped-in music, and electric lights at midday. Often, too, because our work requires travel or relocation as opportunities arise to better our condition in some way, we may feel rootless, cut off from connections with any extended family or a place we think of as home. Late-twentieth-century urban life seems to separate us from one another and from the earth we have sprung from and upon which we depend for our existence. We worry about the effect on us of world overpopulation, the destruction of our environment, and war—all of which will make living more difficult or even somewhat precarious.

The question of how to retain one's sanity, to maintain a state of equanimity, and to be optimistic in the face of insoluble problems and possible annihilation has been with us to a greater or lesser degree for thousands of years. It is not new to our time, although it appears that the problems we face are of greater moment and more encompassing in that they are global instead of merely local and involve far greater numbers of

1

living beings. It might be said, however, that people in past centuries faced threats to their lives and well-being of, to them, equal magnitude. Also, after all, the ending of the world or civilization is an abstraction, because in the thinking of most people the world, as they know it, ends when they do.

If we fear the consequences of the direction in which the world is moving, how can we alter the course of events? Aside from attempting to do something about the world's problems, if we are dissatisfied with our lives, if we are suffering, how can we learn to become content with what we have and reduce our suffering?

Sages have suggested solutions for the problems we face and ways we can change the unwanted conditions of our lives. But, of course, they see the world differently from the way we do. They base their recommendations on their perception of the interconnectedness of all that exists, so that change in one part of the world changes all the other parts. Thus, each of our actions affects the world, if even in a minute way. Further, they believe that the world is a projection or reflection of our minds. It follows that as our minds change, or our thinking alters, our world also will change. It may well be that the world view of the sage is closer to reality than the generally held one.

The ultimate counsel seems to be that we must work on ourselves in order to change the world. The logic is that the kind of person we are, or become, influences everything we do and everyone we encounter. On this note, legend has it that in ancient China rulers welcomed a sage to their domain in the belief that the sage's presence would bring everyone good fortune.

In another sense, if our work on ourselves changes our thought patterns, the world may change for us, because we are seeing it differently. Problems might then be viewed as different in nature or of smaller dimensions than our earlier thinking painted them. They might be considered as merely stage settings and scenarios we have arranged for ourselves to help us unfold or develop.

Predisposed by our acculturation and education, as many of us are, toward doing something concrete to change our world for the better, it is difficult for us to believe that we can solve the problems confronting us

2

unless we meet them actively head on. Such action may take the form of organizing protest meetings and marches, engaging in political action, appointing committees to study a problem and to make recommendations, and raising money to spend on changing an undesirable state of affairs. We may believe that educating people or helping them better themselves materially will improve our world.

These methods and others like them have their uses, but what seems primary in promoting beneficial change is to help people to see the world through different eyes, to give up or go beyond the often limiting and destructive concepts or ideas they acquired as they grew up. Some have termed this transformation "being born again" and through this rebirth to know that the world and all it contains is a part of us and we a part of it. Such a thoroughgoing realization will cause us to think and act in ways that will probably be less harmful to and more nurturing of everything than was our want previously. Moreover, we will influence in a positive way most of the people we meet in our daily lives.

In many methods of working on ourselves the link between the body and the mind is utilized so that the physical movement required in an endeavor is used to affect the mind. One such approach is Asian martial arts training, in which masters teach a particular martial art as a meditative discipline. This book is about the opportunities for developing ourselves this training can provide.

I chose, and advocate, Asian martial arts over Western ones for a number of reasons. First, the Asian arts seem more sophisticated and inclusive than the Western and, therefore, more effective as unarmed fighting systems. More important, their study usually involves practice on more than just the physical level, attempting consciously to include the mental and spiritual. Finally, in a more personal vein, I found very appealing the possibility of getting to know an exotic culture firsthand through a study of one or more of that culture's martial arts.

By contrast, those of our Western forms of combat, like boxing and wrestling, which seem to parallel the Asian arts, have been generally regarded as sportive. It is true that boxing and wrestling are not without their traditions of fair play, fighting spirit, perseverance, and other virtues connected with individual combat. Also, on another level, fighters often

3

experience a feeling of closeness or warmth for their opponent when their bout is over and they have shared the difficult environment of the ring or mat. Those involved in such combative activities in the West can learn from them much more than techniques and methods of besting an opponent, but not if their minds are closed to the possibilities. In studying the Asian martial arts I found that many of their practitioners consciously attempted to go beyond the practical or sportive aspects to those that could help them become more focused, tranquil, mindful, and insightful.

It may well be that as our highly materialistic Western culture becomes more pervasive in the rest of the world, the ability and willingness of students to use martial and other arts to awaken a broader and deeper understanding of themselves and of the world will weaken. Nevertheless, it seems unlikely that this knowledge will ever be lost completely. Attempts at self-realization, though ebbing and flowing with the times, have been perennial.

As for my martial arts experience, I have studied and taught martial arts for over forty years. I began with judo under Yamamoto Yukiso in Hawaii, then studied judo at the Kodokan and karate at the Japan Karate Association in Japan, and finally tai chi chuan with Cheng Man-ching in New York. Along the way I did a bit of aikido in Hawaii and at Uyeshiba's school in Japan, and tried kendo for a short while. Attempting to discover the spiritual underpinnings of the martial arts, I did *zazen* for time at a Soto Zen Buddhist temple in Japan and elsewhere.

The positive changes I observed in myself over the years as I pursued these disciplines, and those I observed in my students, lead me to recommend such practice as a way of seeing oneself and the world more clearly, and of achieving a measure of inner security and tranquillity in a troubled world. In the following chapters I will attempt to set down as concretely as possible what I think practicing the martial arts can give one. In addition, I will try to warn of wrong turnings in this training, of directions that detract from or fail to promote a hoped-for development.

Readers must, however, keep in mind that all I have to say must be tested and explored through their own experience and practice. Answers or solutions to the human predicament cannot be provided by someone else. Nor are they to be found outside ourselves. Someone may point the

4

way, but whatever is there is to be found *within* through alert, diligent, and perseverant application of certain principles over many years. Nor should we expect any final answers but should realize that our training, if correctly done, will slowly but surely develop us to the extent of our capabilities. This is a satisfying and joyful process and is enough.

*Asian names are given last name first.

CHAPTER II

Physical Exercise in Martial Arts

> Those who are more adapted to the active life
> can prepare themselves for contemplation in the
> practice of the active life, while those who are
> more adapted to the contemplative life can take
> upon themselves the works of the active life so
> as to become yet more apt for contemplation.
> ST. THOMAS AQUINAS

SOME THINK OF martial arts as only or mainly physical. They reject the claims their practitioners make for the qualities of mind and spirit developed in those who practice these arts. Those who consider martial arts in this way are almost always people who have no real experience of doing martial arts. Moreover, they are influenced in their thinking by our culture's tendency to divide a functioning whole into parts and to speak of the parts as if they could in some way stand alone and could be understood in this way.

Those who have trained in a martial art for a few years usually begin to sense that there is no separation between the spirit, the mind, and the body. The attempt to separate a part from the whole in order to analyze it may have a certain value, but we must not forget that the essential functioning of a part is to help make the whole what it is. All parts of the whole are interdependent, one part affecting all the others and being in turn affected by them. Thus, the physical movements we perform affect not only our body but every other characteristic of our being. This point of view might form a useful backdrop for a discussion of the physical aspects of martial arts training.

It is true that what strikes us immediately or most forcefully when we are introduced to martial arts training is its physicality. Whether throwing someone in judo, kicking and punching in karate, or applying wrist locks in aikido, a great deal of body movement is involved. In addition to the movements called for by the art, students often do supplementary exercises like running, calisthenics, and weight training.

All this training increases physical strength, agility, and endurance. In addition, our body becomes more muscular and we move about as most athletes usually do—fairly gracefully, well balanced, and with the appearance of strength in reserve. People who like to look this way or who enjoy the feeling of working and playing with a reliable, coordinated, and well-trained body will readily appreciate such benefits.

We should not be misled, however, into thinking that a muscular appearance necessarily signifies good health. It is more in our interest to have a less impressive outer appearance and stronger and more resilient inner organs. On this score those who do martial arts are well served, because this training is aerobic—developing the cardiovascular system and providing our internal organs with the exercise they need to function optimally over a long and active life.

Working with our body in the martial arts allows us to develop coordinated physical movement in which the required muscles are most effectively and efficiently employed. Through seemingly endless drills we learn to establish the most direct pathways for powerful offensive and defensive techniques. (For example, a portion of each judo practice session was devoted to doing repetitions of our favorite throw until we were exhausted. In karate we ran through our repertoire of punches, strikes, and kicks for at least half an hour each day. These drills were done in addition to sparring with an opponent and *kata* (form) practice.) Obviously, our minds must also be employed in learning movement patterns that, at first, feel awkward. The process helps to reinforce and enhance a desirable harmony between mental and physical functioning.

Not all the martial arts need be done strenuously. Those who may dislike strenuous exercise or whose body may have broken down through illness, accident, or age may choose to do a less strenuous martial art like tai chi chuan. In contrast to fighting systems that generally develop muscular strength and are considered hard or "external," tai chi is termed an "internal" system of boxing where we respond to an attack by attempting to be yielding and pliable. Here movements are generally done more slowly and with much less expenditure of energy than in the other martial arts. Although cardiovascular fitness and muscular development conferred by training in these internal arts will not equal those of the more strenuously pursued harder ones, students will nevertheless become appreciably stronger and fitter.

As we become more skillful in our martial art, we learn to move in a relaxed way. If our body is tense and stiff, our moves will be slow and seem inhibited and restricted. We attempt to loosen those muscles not necessary to an action so that the muscles actually used are permitted to function fully and explosively. One way to learn to relax is to be forced to perform close to the point of exhaustion. For example, when I began training in judo, I had to learn to fall correctly by being thrown repeatedly until I became so tired that I could hardly stand. At this juncture my falls actually improved and it became almost a pleasure to fly through the air before landing and having to rise again. By contrast, at the outset of each session's falling practice my tendency was to tense up in anticipation of landing on the mat. This tensing was unintentional, sometimes made my fall painful, was not conducive to countering the throw when I reached that stage, but occurred nonetheless.

Learning to relax is clearly very useful in our everyday life. The psychological stress in our lives often exceeds the optimum necessary for a zestful life. The more strenuous martial arts help us to release the tensions we develop in our fast-paced world by draining us of built-up energy or by allowing us to expend it in a controlled way. If we have no release for this excessive stress, it can begin to undermine our health. After a practice session we usually feel pleasantly tired and at peace with ourselves and the world. This good feeling might also be the product of certain internal bodily chemical reactions to sustained hard physical effort. Exercise physiologists have demonstrated the role of endorphins in producing a "high" in runners and other endurance athletes.

Practicing a martial art like tai chi chuan can teach us to relax by the constant emphasis on using the minimum of energy to perform an action and also on learning to offer no resistance to an attack. We defend ourselves by presenting the opponent with a target to attack (an area of our body), neutralizing the attack by withdrawing the target (no resistance), and counterattacking as the opponent, expecting to make contact with the target, overextends and loses balance. The object of this tai chi training, and of all training for that matter, is to internalize the principles involved in the art. Thus, we gradually learn to go about our daily business in a relaxed and settled way, and attempt to deflect or neutralize attacks, or an opposing force of whatever nature, by not resisting. Offering no resistance is not merely to give up but to flexibly bend without breaking so the attack loses its force and fails to accomplish its intended objective. How exactly to do this in the often complicated interactions we have with others needs a great deal of experience. But, at the least, employing the principle of nonresistance in our lives is more promising than trying to force people and events into a form we favor and becoming unyielding in response to opposition.

If we can internalize this more relaxed attitude, it may then be unnecessary to practice more strenuously, despite the desirability of the benefits conferred by harder practice. The tension that modern urban life seems to generate in almost everyone will not be completely absent, but it will be there to a lesser degree. An easier, more flexible frame of mind will also help us to see that there are many events over which we can exercise little direct control. Moreover, our tendency to control others, to expect them to behave in a way we think correct, will diminish. We may also learn to be easier and more reasonable in our expectations of ourselves.

My own training has usually included some form of strenuous activity. Those of my students who have practiced only tai chi for many years, however, seem to continue in good health and general well-being. Thus, as stated above, it may be unnecessary to tax the body further than is demanded by the movements in the tai chi form and tai chi push-hands, provided that this practice is a daily routine.

At any rate, in my experience, an hour or two of moving practice, even if quite strenuous in nature, seemed to give me more energy during the rest of the day than if I failed to practice. A strenuous workout usually included a two-mile jog, followed by elements of karate, judo, and aikido training with a partner, and ending with a few exercises to develop strength—like parallel bar dips and horizontal bar chinups. If a problem in my life seemed to defy solution, this workout changed my perspective on it or released the tension built up by my searching for answers or imagining an unwanted outcome. Invariably, I felt good—more relaxed and more optimistic after practice than before.

In my earlier book, *The Martial Spirit,* I wrote of the legendary Buddhist monk Bodhidharma, who brought elements of Buddhism from India to China. Finding the monks at the Shaolin Temple in poor physical condition and believing that this deficiency would detract from their mental and spiritual growth, he introduced a number of martial exercises. These movements became the foundation of Shaolin Temple Kung Fu, a famous fighting style throughout China.

The value for us of good physical conditioning in all of our endeavors seems without question. There is no doubt that the energy we have to give to the pursuit of our interests will be greater if we are physically healthy and in good condition. Thus, the martial exercises referred to—done with proper direction and concentration—probably helped the monks attain their mental and spiritual realizations.

As concerns mental and spiritual considerations, which we will discuss more fully in the following chapters, it is quite possible that an optimistic outlook toward our life and toward the world, the feeling that we live in a benign universe, need not derive from reasoned and logical argument. Nor might it have to come from mental and spiritual training that purports to allow us to break through surface appearance to underlying reality. Perhaps an optimistic outlook is merely the effect on our system—in all its physical, mental, and spiritual aspects—of properly conducted physical training over the years.

CHAPTER III

Self-Defense in Martial Arts

> "He abused me, he beat me, he defeated me, he robbed me"—in those who harbor such thoughts hatred will never cease.
>
> "He abused me, he beat me, he defeated me, he robbed me"—in those who do not harbor such thoughts hatred will cease.
>
> For hatred does not cease by hatred at any time—this is an old rule.
>
> DHAMMAPADA

OVER THE YEARS many students have come to my classes to learn to defend themselves. Some had been attacked on the street. Others had experienced verbal threats and confrontations that might have ended in physical violence. They sought an overall security or at least the feeling of confidence in their ability to handle an actual or potential assailant. In our training, I have usually attempted to deemphasize preparation for fighting in favor of other aspects. I have advised engaging in the art for its own sake, letting it affect all areas of our being however it will.

My reasons for downplaying self-defense in the martial arts classes I teach spring from a number of consideratons. To begin with, I have been especially taken with the thought and the experience that things are not what they seem. I may have been drawn toward this point of view by my contact with Buddhist ideas, which maintain that life is illusion.

This philosophical position receives additional support from what I know of the mechanics of politics and the world of microphysics. Here surface appearance is far from underlying reality. An opportunity to live for some years in another culture also strongly influenced my thinking. It gradually became evident that people there did not, in general, share the American view of life. There seems to be not one correct world view but instead many different and equally valid ways of living life. Thus, the conduct of human affairs and the fundamental makeup of the world are not what surface appearance would indicate, and are far more complicated than we think.

In addition, on a more personal level, I believe we lack awareness of and understanding about the reason we are in our particular everyday environment, whatever it may be. I think we choose our environment and that we are not where we are by accident. This choice is usually only partly a conscious one and is made mainly on other levels of the mind. The reason for our choice of a situation is probably to experience it and to learn from it. Further, we attract whatever happens to us because we intentionally, though not necessarily consciously, open ourselves to the event. Those who cannot accept this theory might attempt, through psychoanalysis or some other means of knowing themselves better, to try to get at the root causes of some disaster or something which seems to have "happened" to them.

These suggestions that our idea of how the world works may be mistaken or distorted should at least give us pause about giving quick, ready-made, and facile explanations for anything we do. We might then try to look beneath the surface to try to understand the more basic or underlying reasons for how we act with other people or interact with the rest of the world. More to the point for our discussion, we might question why we feel we need to study a martial art mainly in order to learn to defend ourselves.

It is likely that the desire for enhanced self-defense ability stems from a feeling of insecurity. If we have experienced a physical encounter on the street or with an acquaintance in which we came off second-best, we might wish to strengthen ourselves or learn how to fight so that in the future we will beat our adversary instead of being beaten. It is also possible that we may lack confidence in ourselves in a general way and think that if we are trained to fight we will develop and project a stronger personality. Perhaps we wish to increase our personal power in order to dominate or control others.

14

We may wish to learn self-defense for all these reasons as well as for others I have not mentioned. But usually learning a martial art for self-defense—even if we recognize our insecurity, lack of self-confidence, or desire for power over others—is still only a surface expression of deeper needs or problems that require solution. Because these deeper problems are not solved simply by learning self-defense, those who join martial arts classes with only the intention to learn self-defense usually stay for only a short time. Often what is taught requires much more of a commitment of effort and perseverance than was anticipated. New students may have thought that a few lessons, or investing a few evenings a week for six months at the most, would be sufficient to confer fighting ability and all they hoped for from this. When they realize that adequate fighting skills require a few years of training, many conclude that the results will not be worth the effort.

Because the emphasis in most martial arts is not on learning to fight in the street, even those who train for a few years may still feel inadequately prepared for a brawl. Quite competent fighters, too, can imagine a situation that begins as an unarmed confrontation and escalates as an adversary produces a knife or a gun. Unarmed fighting skill may be insufficient to cope with these weapons. Should they then also learn to shoot accurately, become expert with edged weapons, and carry a gun or a knife in order to feel safe? Should the gun be an automatic weapon so that they are the equal in firepower of anyone they may chance to meet? What if they are outnumbered?

This progression may seem to carry the argument to absurdity, but the point is that we can never feel completely confident of our ability to defend ourselves even if we are highly skilled. In my own case, the desire to become strong and to develop the ability to defend myself in an unarmed confrontation were certainly factors in my choosing to study martial arts. But as I began to see what constituted the judo I studied at the outset of my career, I soon developed a different perspective. The Kodokan judo I learned in Hawaii in the late forties and early fifties had more of the flavor of learning a way of life. Self-defense was a minor aspect of our training.

The karate I studied in Japan from 1956 to 1958 might be thought of more as a fighting art, but here, too, training focused on gaining a kind of self-realization through hard practice. Moreover, the eight years of judo

15

I had done before beginning karate had already conditioned me to think of martial arts training as a pursuit that included mental and spiritual aspects as much as the physical.

The question might be asked, however, whether or not my enhanced fighting ability over the years protected me from harm or whether there were occasions on which I had to use my skills to defend myself. This is difficult to answer because I'm sure that my training had an effect on my body so that I looked strong and in good shape. Also, I probably projected an aura of confidence that may have discouraged potential attackers. Yet, I believe that the few situations I encountered that required a physical response could have been satisfactorily concluded even if I had had no fighting skill.

Let us examine, in a bit more detail, the issue of self-defense and of fighting. When we begin martial arts training, our teachers, if they are reputable, impress upon us that we must not use our skills outside the *dojo* (training hall). Students who fight on the street are warned against indulging in such behavior, and if they fail to control themselves are expelled. Thus, we are taught that even when an opportunity to fight presents itself we are to walk away from it. This is not always easy to do, because we might feel cowardly when we back away from a situation that might become violent. Also, our friends or loved ones might have a different outlook from ours about what constitutes desirable behavior in a confrontation. We may be thrust into a fight because we have to satisfy the aggressiveness or hostility of someone close to us or because we are unable or unwilling to face the recriminations from this person attendant on our failure to take a "proper" stand. We might have to fight, also, if we go to dangerous neighborhoods where the likelihood of encountering trouble is great.

Partly by good fortune—although what happens to us is almost never simply the result of chance—I have been able to escape fighting, except for almost minor engagements of little consequence. This is true despite my working for more than a year for a few nights a week as a bouncer in an Oakland, California, dance hall where liquor was served, and for a couple of weeks at a bar on Guam. Generally, I avoided fights by trying to stay away from places where they were likely to occur, by keeping a

16

generally low profile, and by staying alert, trying to spot trouble early enough to be able to move away from it or to defuse it before it blew up. When I chose an environment where violence was likely, as in the dance hall and bar, I found that the skill required in almost all my dealings with unruly customers was the ability to verbally prevail on them to leave and sometimes to soothe their ruffled feelings. As stated above, I must not discount, however, the effect on these customers, as well as on other people, of my appearing competent and physically strong. A related point is that I was reasonably large and strong-looking enough to discourage frivolous attacks, yet not so large as to offer a challenge to those who might want to prove that they are not intimidated by another person's size.

Appearing to others as a formidable adversary need not depend on our learning self-defense or practicing fighting. Though such persons are rare, those who have a determined nature and little fear of personal injury or of losing their lives will send out signals that they are best left alone. Muggers, for example, assess potential victims by the latters' body language: their walk or the set of their body. Secondly, if we do find ourselves having to fight, a fierce determination and a willingness, especially for the smaller and weaker, to use as a weapon whatever comes to hand can achieve a satisfactory result. Finally, whether in physical or nonphysical confrontation, a clever fighter will choose the ground and circumstances favorable to him or her and unfavorable to the adversary. An extreme example of such a choice is the surprise attack or the ambush. Seemingly, much of the fighting between rival interests in the old west was not of the kind in which has antagonists shooting it out face to face on the main street at high noon, but of enemies shooting from ambush, taking as little personal risk as possible.

In any event, martial arts training offers us more than advantageous fighting techniques and practice in using them. Other aspects of training receive much more emphasis when these arts are taught, or considered, not in a shallow or narrow way but as a preparation for living more fully and completely. The gradual outcome of such training can be the formation in us of a different view of life, one in which we begin to see through some of the illusion that clouds or obscures our vision. Competitiveness, the need to outdo others, and the anxiety attendant on the possibility of

17

failure in our endeavors usually become of decreasing concern. Insecurity, which may give rise in us to a desire for a way to defend ourselves from physical attack, can slowly give way to a belief that the universe is generally benign and well ordered. We will discover in ourselves a willingness to meet events spontaneously with whatever mental and physical resources we possess. We may also see that the ultimate outcome of whatever we do is of far less importance than the process of doing whatever we do in each moment to the best of our ability.

This does not mean that we will never meet a situation in which we decide to fight. But perhaps our development will allow us to realize that we have pulled the event to us, that it did not just happen. If we wish to know why we attracted a violent situation, this knowledge can be brought into our consciousness. Such a mental exercise can, for example, reveal that we wanted to experience directly the excitement and danger, the feelings of victory or defeat, and even the possible injury and loss of life. But if this was our choice, we could have fought whether we prepared for it by learning some measure of self-defense or simply used to the full whatever mental and physical equipment we had.

Some have suggested that we can solve the problem of self-defense by deciding to live nonviolently. Yet we cannot live completely nonviolently and stay alive. In fact, life abounds in the food we eat, the air we breathe, and the water we drink. Many organisms are destroyed when we take them into our body. It seems that nonviolence can only be embraced in some degree rather than absolutely. Accepting this limitation on our ability to live completely without violence may make it easier for us to pursue our interests, as we accept the fact that this pursuit cannot help but bring us into some conflict with others. But if we begin to shed some of the illusions of our society and are selective about our choice of interests, we may decide to engage in activities that are thought to be of benefit to most people or at least not harmful and we will, therefore, suffer less opposition. Also, by recognizing the destructiveness to ourselves and others of an over-weening personal ambition, we may be able to reduce this drive in our lives, making us seem less threatening to others. We may gradually discover that we do not want the material things or the status that others want from life, or we may find ourselves content with relatively little. This way of living usually gives others the feeling that we are a nonthreatening and fairly harmless human being, although some may consider us inconsequential, eccentric, or stupid. Where our pursuits do encounter opposition we should bring to bear whatever judgment, discernment, and wisdom we have developed in an effort to win over our adversaries or to make some creative and, to them, more attractive change in the mix that consitutes the situation. As a last resort, we may decide to avoid violence by accepting a less than satisfactory situation or by removing ourselves from a hostile environment to a friendlier one.

An interesting and instructive discussion about an individual's wrestling with himself over the issue of his participaton in war, and of course, in hurting and killing others, occurs in the Hindu epic poem *Bhagavad-gita*. In the *Gita* a great warrior, Arjuna, speaks with his god, Krishna, just before a battle between two opposing forces. Arjuna, recognizing respected kinsmen and teachers among the foe, feels his strength ebbing and in despair tells Krishna that no reward would be great enough for him to kill these "enemies." Killing them, he says, would be an act of evil far greater than the evil they are supposed to embody. It would be better just to submit and let them kill him.

Krishna replies, in essence, that Arjuna does not see clearly, that Brahman, or the Atman, the Godhead that is within all creatures and things, cannot be destroyed. The Atman that possesses the body is eternal. It is delusion to think that we are the destroyers or that we are destroyed. Krishna advises Arjuna to do his duty as a warrior, to fight wholeheartedly in a righteous war, and to support those who depend upon him. Otherwise he will be considered disgraced, thought to be refusing to fight out of fear and be spoken of as a coward through the ages, a sad fate for a man of honor.

The *Gita* is, of course, part of Hindu religious literature. As with all religious literature, it contains hints of reality, of what underlies the world that appears to our senses. At the same time, such literature is the product of a culture, written by culturally conditioned persons and usually subject to the approval of that culture's rulers. Therefore, the writing will express the culture's attitudes toward life, though it may attempt to base its prescriptions for social behavior on the insights of its seers or wise men.

Thus, Krishna's advice to Arjuna to fight without qualms in a righteous war certainly might be questioned. Righteousness is a difficult concept to judge and to apply, especially where societies with different aims, interests, and outlooks find themselves in opposition to one another. If they go to war, each society will think of itself as fighting a righteous war. To survive, societies must believe their cause is just and that their interests should be served. Moreover, the society's warriors cannot be permitted the luxury of deciding whether or not to fight, lest such vacillation cause weakness, resulting in defeat and perhaps annihilation.

In our modern era, these issues may no longer really exist, because our weapons are now of such awesome power that were they used our world, or at least the civilization we know, would be destroyed. Waging war with such weapons would seem out of the question. Thus, if the concept of righteousness is recognized as containing a good measure of self-interest, we might realize that we cannot engage in warfare, at least not on a grand scale, and might be better advised to work at cooperation and at living amicably together. It is true that people of different cultures see the world differently, but we must try to discover what is basically or universally desirable for all human beings, and even for all living creatures, and to hold to this in our dealings with one another. Such a course probably seems overly naive and expectations from following it overly optimistic. Yet this course, while not easy or productive of quick results, seems much to be preferred to courses based on the premise that other societies are evil and must be suppressed or destroyed.

On the other hand, if the leaders of an opposing society have aggressive aims, believing that the threat or reality of warfare will secure them economic or other advantage, a strong defense to deter the possibility of their attempting an adventurous foray is also essential. Usually, when two or more societies are in conflict the roots of such conflict can be traced to prior mistakes stemming from decades of narrow self-interest. Perhaps we can correct these past mistakes and work toward greater cooperation, knowing that the spoils of war are no longer an incentive, because nuclear warfare would not only make spoils nonexistent but deprive us of what we already have.

It sometimes seems that limited warfare might be profitable, but even limited warfare has wider repercussions than we anticipate. The situation in the Middle East, for instance, is far from a simple matter of the United States–led UN checking a ruthless dictator in his attempt to dominate his neighbors. Beneath the surface we can discern the ferment of all sorts of political, economic, and religious elements, ranging from control of oil to the centuries-old fierce antagonism between Islam and other religions. Thus, a deeper and broader perspective on these problems will cause us to question the value of even limited warfare for our long-term interests.

Moving again to our personal concern with the issue of violence, suppose we agree that divinity resides in every creature, that it cannot be destroyed, and that both pleasure and pain are transitory. May we then, because it doesn't really matter, hurt and kill other creatures? Some would say that violence is justified if our cause is just. But even on a personal level identifying a just cause seems very difficult. Almost all of us believe we are doing or trying to do the right thing. Recognizing this should make us wary of coming to a conclusion about what is just, especially if our conclusion leads to violence. Whether or not we accept the concepts of karma and reincarnation, we must also remember that even if we cannot kill the godhead in another person, if we physically or mentally injure someone, we are causing that person pain and other upset, transitory though such feelings may be.

Still another view of the subject is found in theories that suggest that it is to our advantage to undergo certain kinds of physical and mental hardship, especially at the hands of another person. This difficult period in our lives can strengthen us mentally and spiritually. These theories advocate our living as spiritual warriors, following a course that can open us to enlightenment. To live in this way we must be aware of what we are doing, aware that we have chosen our predicament and are using it to further our spiritual aims.

On the other hand, we may choose to act violently if we do not want to suffer violence at someone else's hands or submit to the will of someone who seeks to dominate us, to take what we have, or to violate us or those who depend on us. Though we may have failed to notice the approach of violence and, therefore, admitted it into our life, it seems more in keeping with the life force within us to fight back to the best of our ability when we have to protect ourselves and those we feel responsible for. If we find ourselves in this situation we might console ourselves with the thought that we have probably chosen this role for some purpose, though we may not be conscious of the choice and must simply act appropriately to defend what we believe are our interests.

I should add some final words concerning people who are drawn to a career in the military or in law enforcement. They have selected an environment where violence is common, and if they wish to remain there to learn what it can teach them, they would be well advised to develop a high level of armed and unarmed combat skills, as well as outstanding physical condition. Such skills and conditioning are not only for their individual benefit. Because they must often function as members of a team, their skills also serve to support their fellow officers when danger threatens. In addition, they cannot, at a crucial point, take time to consider the pros and cons of "right" action or be unwilling to use necessary force. It is not unusual for them to meet a situation where inaction or evasion is less desirable, or far more dangerous, than taking the initiative and attacking.

Yet, even in these difficult circumstances, they can take measures to enable them to make their effect on those with whom they must interact a more positive one. Though it may not appear so to the criminal they have arrested, talking him into surrendering is preferable to physically subduing him and successfully applying an unarmed combat technique is preferable to shooting. Learning appropriate martial arts, which means ongoing training over the years, confers the confidence and the physical bearing that must underlie any attempt at persuasion. Training develops the alertness that allows an officer to notice signs of impending trouble early enough to head it off or to prepare countermeasures. Unarmed combat training can reduce reliance on firearms so that the injuries inflicted will usually be minor or less severe.

It seems clear that focusing on self-defense does not really address, let alone solve, the problems that stem from violence in ourselves and in our daily lives. The foregoing theories may allow us to formulate more realistic ways of coming to terms with violence.

It seems unnecessary for most of us to study the martial arts in order to defend ourselves from unexpected physical attack. These arts have much more to offer us than effective fighting techniques. If we focus on the elements in the martial arts that seem unrelated to fighting, we will gain benefits of a kind that bear more directly on what our lives are all about. As for personal security, wisdom may well lie in recognizing that it cannot be achieved to the extent many of us, mistakenly, think is necessary to our welfare.

CHAPTER IV

Meditational Aspects of Martial Arts

> A stream at the mountain's foot flows down ceaselessly.
> When the meditating mind is like this, seeing into one's
> own nature will not be far away.
>
> HAKUIN EKAKU

IN THE LAST decade or two, the popular press has run articles extolling the positive effects on our physical and mental health of a daily period of meditation. Twenty to thirty minutes daily of some kind of meditation practice is said to calm and quiet us, to release tension and reduce stress.

We can meditate in all sorts of ways, ranging from doing the tasks of everyday life in a mindful way to sitting without moving, noting each of our inhalations and exhalations. We can try to still our conscious mind by watching the successive rise and fall of our thoughts. Alternatively, we can fully occupy the conscious mind by concentrating on repeating a mantra (words or phrases designed to bring us to a higher state of consciousness), viewing mandalas (pictures or diagrams that help open our mind), doing breathing exercises, or struggling with a koan (a spiritual exercise in which we attempt to achieve insight into a seemingly incomprehensible verbal formulation pointing at ultimate truth), to name a few.

Many who meditate do so for more than stress reduction, calming, or general health reasons. But if "health" is more broadly interpreted as including, or even dependent on, spiritual development, then meditators might be said to engage in meditation for this broader purpose. This practice is said to help us to fashion the mind into an instrument capable of the kind of concentrated effort that will enable us to see ourselves and the world with greater clarity. It is also held that when we control and quiet the conscious mind, we can hear the voice of our more intuitive nature. Our intuition contains valuable knowledge and wisdom concerning our place in the world and our connection with everything.

At first glance, martial arts practice does not appear to be meditation. *Kata*, or form practice, may look like a dance, and practice with a partner may look like a competition or a violent encounter. What seems to make an activity meditative is the way we use the mind in its pursuit. Thus, where a martial art is taught as a meditative discipline, students are urged to invest their thoughts fully in what they are doing. An extraneous thought may intrude but is ignored in favor of continued concentration on the unfolding action. In practice with an opponent, mental lapses, or the mind's straying from the requirements of attack and defense, are discouraged not only by our attempt to follow instructions but by the knowledge, periodically reinforced, that the opponent's successful attack could bring pain and even injury.

As stated above, my introduction to martial arts came through the practice of judo in Hawaii in the 1940s. I was not looking for training in meditation when I started judo, but for knowledge about and skill in fighting. The esoteric and exotic aspect of judo, the product of an Eastern culture, also attracted me. At that time, the East seemed even more mysterious to the West than it is today. My teacher, Yamamoto Yukiso, was Japanese and taught the Kodokan judo he had learned in Japan. The flavor of the training was what I later learned to know as Japanese. The atmosphere in the training hall was serious, formal, and austere. Although the idea was seldom discussed, we got the impression that much more was involved in our training than just the physical act of throwing and grappling. We implicitly were made aware that we were doing something that trained the mind and spirit as well as the body. The training seemed intended to develop us as human beings on more than one level.

It was taken for granted that it was necessary to focus the mind fully if we were to be successful in our attacking and defending. Nothing was said about having to act in the moment with no thought of past and future, but upon reflection we might have noticed that we were doing this. We were not told to think of nothing and to simply react as the situation

26

demanded, but we found that playing judo contrary to this principle reduced our effectiveness. For example, our opponent did not always move in the way we might have anticipated, leaving a small gap in the smooth flow of our functioning as we were forced to let go of our misdirected focus. An alert opponent sensed opportunity in such a gap.

Some fifteen years elapsed before I embarked on more formal meditation. During these years I became familiar with the idea that Zen Buddhism is an important underpinning of Japanese culture and Japanese martial arts. Wanting to find out for myself what *zazen* could give me, I spent some months in Japan pursuing this discipline. Although I did not very much like the motionless and uncomfortable sitting and watching my breath, its effects contributed to a quieting of my mind and persuaded me that *zazen* should be a part of my life. Consequently, off and on over the years, I did mornng *zazen* for twenty to thirty minutes. While *zazen* was beneficial, my major training emphasis centered on judo, karate, and tai chi; I would have to attribute my development or insights largely to these disciplines.

Some masters of meditative discipline have stated that only by following their methods could we hope to break the hold on our minds of illusion or delusion. Their belief may well stem from their concentration on their own discipline and the tendency for masters to think most efficacious what they know best. Other masters have expressed their beliefs on this matter less rigidly by saying that disciplines other than theirs might give us a certain level or degree of realization but only training in theirs would bestow *full* realization. In my experience, breakthroughs to a new or different way of seeing the world can come in any number of ways and not necessarily even by following a particular discipline. As for degrees of realization, I cannot help thinking that such gradations are very difficult to establish or assess.

At any rate, there is no question in my mind that the martial arts training I have undergone over the years has served as meditation. I might even say that I feel that the moving meditation we do in martial arts has advantages over sitting meditation. But this feeling probably derives from my particular makeup or my personal inclination. There is really no need to make a comparison between moving and sitting still in meditation. We can do either or both with good results.

In martial arts we can meditate doing individual *kata* or while practicing with an opponent. But it is probably useful and perhaps even necessary to study with a teacher who sees martial arts training as meditative if we are to embark on the right path at the outset. If we practice at a club or school where the emphasis in training is on learning to fight or on sport, we may experience considerable delay, or fail altogether, in developing ourselves to the degree or in the manner we desire. Of course, in practical terms, we usually gravitate toward a teacher whose approach to life or state of development accords with or reflects our own. If we want to practice martial arts in order to become more powerful, to gain advantage over others, or merely for the good feeling we get from a physical workout, we will have little trouble in finding a teacher to help us achieve those purposes. But even if our interests lie primarily in a less traveled direction, we will sooner or later find someone to point the way.

If we are following a more meditative approach in our individual form practice, we will learn to become increasingly focused on the moves we are making. Doing the tai chi form, especially, lends itself to learning to focus on what we are doing, because we do the movements slowly. Compared with performing a much faster karate *kata*, we are given more chance to notice the rise of thoughts in our consciousness and to learn to allow them to disappear without being caught by them. In addition, physical and mental relaxation seems easier to achieve, or is given greater emphasis, in tai chi than is true in what are considered "harder" or "external" martial arts. Yet the form practice in all the martial arts can teach us to concentrate and to focus so that we can be fully in the moment.

Functioning fully in each moment depends on concentration, but also goes beyond it to an attempt at trying to live our lives in a direct, spontaneous way. Our everyday actions are usually diluted by thoughts of the past and the future. When we eat, hold a conversation, or work at something, we are not completely there if our minds are preoccupied with some worry or the anticipation of a desirable future event. Thus, the flavor of the moment, of concrete experience is diluted by abstractions.

Practicing with an opponent can be meditative in the same way as doing the individual form. But here we notice an additional complication: it might seem that our opponent is not helping but is trying to hinder our meditation. The opponent could be aggressive or bent on hurting us, and at the very least has interests opposed to ours. He or she will be trying to throw, hit, kick, or push us and we are trying to avoid the attack and to attack in turn. To maintain our focus, to be unaffected mentally by the interaction characteristic of this rather highly charged encounter, is very difficult. We must learn to ignore all irrelevant stimuli, such as whether we are winning or losing, disappointment with our efforts, or how we may appear to someone who is observing us, to mention a few. We must simply try to do the best we can and, above all, keep our minds clear and ready to respond instantaneously whenever we sense the necessity. A particular advantage of this kind of practice is that our opponent's attack, occasioned by his sensing our lapse of attention, will quickly jerk our mind back to the business at hand. Unfortunately, our momentary inattention may have created an irremediable breakdown in our defense, allowing the opponent to defeat us.

Two opponents who are trying their best to defeat each other might seem unable to reach a meditative state, but this condition can by degrees be achieved. It is possible that only one of the two is trying to practice meditatively and will get the benefits of this approach. In such a case, the opponent who does not share the approach will still be to some extent positively affected by his adversary's manner of practicing.

It is easy to see the value of being able to behave with others in our everyday life as we do when we are practicing meditatively with an opponent in the *dojo*. We then will try to function to the best of our ability in each moment without the intrusion of irrelevant thoughts or concern about the final outcome. Of course, many other considerations enter each picture, but this basic way of functioning should stand us in good stead in whatever we do.

When we practice martial arts our teacher may often remind us to move from the area below the navel—the *tan tien*, or *tanden*. This area is considered a reservoir of *chi*, or *ki*, the energy that flows through us and through whatever exists. The result of this emphasis will be to lower our body's center and to help us function in a more settled and grounded way. Naturally, as we practice with an opponent we cannot literally have our mind on the *tan tien*. This focus is gradually achieved as we consciously work

29

on perfecting our form in *kata* or in various controlled sparring or technique-sharpening skills.

The effect on the way we think and feel as our center drops is that we are somehow made aware of knowledge possessed by a part of the body other than the brain. This knowledge is a product of mankind's development over millions of years and it consists of a sense of our connection with other forms of life and with the spirit that infuses everything. Over the millennia men have written of the importance of the *tan tien*, of focusing on it in meditative practice, and of how wisdom, and a more realistic understanding of our existence, can come to us through such practice. We may not be able to articulate the knowledge we gain—or really already have—but we apprehend it as an intuitive feeling. The feeling becomes stronger and more pronounced as we give our attention to the *tan tien* in our training and, perhaps more important, in our daily lives.

The way we live and the rules and patterns we follow in our thinking in modern times, especially in the West, seem to cut us off from this ancient knowledge. Human beings seem always to have tried to construct models of the universe and sought to understand, and perhaps to establish, man's place in it. This urge has many roots, but chief among them may be our fear of annihilation, with the consequent need to learn to work in harmony with the environment or control it. Some cultures have looked to the stars for guidance, attempting to apply to earthly endeavors the designs they detected in the larger realm of the heavens. But others have listened to individuals in their society whose inward vision seemed to provide a measure of understanding and predictability about people and the life around them. Often a culture's choice of the particular model of how things work excludes any other model, so that anyone with an opposing point of view is ignored, considered insane, or even persecuted. We have chosen the scientific method as our way of trying to understand life and most of us tend to dismiss as superstition or worse "unscientific" methods for gaining knowledge and truth.

This attitude is understandable given the role of cultural conditioning in our lives and the part science has played in expanding knowledge and in developing the technology that seems to improve our lot. Nevertheless, a look at today's world does not reveal a particularly happy state of affairs. Many of us have become far less sanguine or confident about the possibility of technology solving our world problems than was true only a few decades ago. We see also that as scientists probe deeper into the workings of nature, they encounter situations and problems that orthodox methods cannot understand or solve. For example, in microphysics the particles or waves physicists encounter behave in ways unaccounted for by traditional physics.

Scientists are becoming increasingly aware of the complexity and interrelatedness of everything in the world. Moreover, while they are finding out more and more about the surface of things, what really makes things work or gives them life continues to be as elusive as ever. Of course, research into more fundamental questions is seldom funded. In today's world the large amounts of money required for research in any area are granted to projects that are generally oriented toward short-term gains that will increase our power or produce profit. Then, too, scientists prefer to work on problems they believe they can solve rather than on those that seem to defy solution.

It is interesting that scientists working in areas of research like microphysics find themselves describing the world in the way mystics have always described it. Such descriptions may lack precision, see phenomena in the world as somewhat unpredictable, and sense at the heart of things a possibly unfathomable mystery. Reflections on these facts may well encourage us to conclude that we are personally capable of apprehending this kind of reality, at least to the degree spoken of by mystics. We have mental faculties that can be sharpened and enhanced through training to the point where we see more deeply into life's processes. We need not depend for our idea of what our life is about and what the world is about on experts or limit ourselves to the parameters of scientific knowledge as they currently exist. The knowledge we can gather from looking inward need not be considered suspect simply because it fails to accord with traditional scientific thinking, which itself is undergoing great change. Neither should we rely completely on our intuitive sense of things. We should probably seek a balanced synthesis between the intuitive and the rational. We should consider looking inward as another way to gain knowledge and understanding, a method we should not neglect because people in our culture, generally, focus their attention outward.

Although we may begin meditating in the hope that doing so will improve our lives or allow us to live more fully and completely, our real interests will be better served if we do not expect anything from meditation. This is not to say that we will get nothing from it. But whatever realizations do come are, in a sense, gifts. There is no guarantee that if we sit for a certain period each day, practice breath control, repeat a mantra, engage in moving meditation or whatever that we will get "it." Why, then, should we meditate? Because it feels right, because including a period of meditation in our daily life seems to ground us, to put us in touch with ourselves and the spirit that infuses all of life.

The all-pervasive information media, the work we do, what we read and study, with whom we associate, and the way we conduct our lives all affect how we see ourselves and what we believe to be true. But our daily period of meditation, in which the conscious mind is stilled for a time, can influence us out of proportion to the time we spend on it. It can allow the upwelling from somewhere within us of what we sense are undeniably true ideas about ourselves and about life.

32

CHAPTER V

Interactions Between Teacher and Students

> If thou shouldst say, "It is enough, I have reached perfection," all is lost. For it is the function of perfection to make one know one's imperfection.
> St. Augustine

LET US ASSUME that we are in a *dojo* where many students, having read or heard that the martial arts constitute an avenue to self-realization, train in the hope that they will learn more than fighting skills. They will attempt to regard the subject matter taught not just in its surface physical appearance but as a means of helping them to become more insightful. Their expectations of their teacher will be high, most wishing to think of him as a special person who has developed to the extent of being able to offer them a method of breaking through delusions to a more enlightened view of themselves and the world.

A disturbing factor often enters this picture when students, even though cautioned against making such judgments, believe they can define and recognize certain desirable mental and spiritual qualities and expect to discover these in their teacher. They may look for the teacher's renunciation of worldly success and of material concerns or believe his interpersonal relations should be of a certain order. But beginners usually judge with their everyday rational minds, without the insight years of training might confer. They employ in their judgment the very delusive thinking they are trying to transcend. Their mistaken early efforts to assess their teacher's qualities, often deriving from a lack of sufficient confidence in themselves or in their teacher's abilities, may lead students to various unproductive positions, ranging from teacher veneration to disillusionment with him and with what he is trying to teach.

At one extreme, veneration of a teacher may have its roots in a wish to believe that he is so highly developed as to possess in his makeup elements that our culture assigns to deity, and that he is then different from the rest of us. The divinity that may be evident in the teacher is, however, in each of us and we are, then, all of us special in that way. Possibly, also, students may revere a teacher simply because they believe he is capable of conferring on them understanding or enlightenment.

At the other extreme are students whose reservations about their training extend to deep doubts about their ability to develop, to break the hold of their conditioning and see themselves and the world differently or with additional clarity. These students may try to find substance or a basis for their doubts in the way their teacher conducts their training and in the way he behaves in the training hall and in everyday life.

Still other students will try to make their teacher into the kind of person they believe he should be. They will discern in him qualities they think he should have and refuse to recognize those they consider negative or inappropriate. My tai chi teacher, Cheng Man-ching, had the look of a Chinese sage and was cast in that role by many of his students who, favoring the counterculture of the middle sixties, sought a mature and wise teacher from the seemingly less materialistic and more spiritual East. This need tended to obscure their seeing Cheng as a real person, with the often inconsistent positive and negative qualities we all have.

Some students may attempt to determine a teacher's qualities and abilities by the way the members of the teacher's family have turned out. Perhaps they will scrutinize his relationship with his wife, if he has one, in an effort to see whether living with him has affected her in a positive way. If he has children, students may wonder in what way they have benefited by having had him as a father. Here, again, some of these students will invest members of the teacher's family with what they consider to be desirable qualities, while others may look for deficiencies and defects.

Trying to determine a teacher's worth by assessing the degree of development achieved by the members of his family is usually misguided.

By what criteria can we judge these family members? If we judge with an undeveloped or deluded mind, we are again faced with the possibility that we are not seeing clearly and that what we think of as desirable accomplishments or qualities may really be illusions. We may be unable either to grasp what constitutes real accomplishment in another person or, if it is there, to detect it, especially when that person makes little effort to demonstrate it. I am reminded here of the Japanese concept of *shibui*, which can be applied to many aspects of life, ranging from the fashioning and manufacture of wearing apparel to the way a person conducts his affairs. An example may be a coat that at first glance looks quite drab and ordinary in color, design, and construction. Closer inspection, however, reveals rather intricate color and design patterns in the weave, as well as the use of material of the highest quality. If our eyes are not open enough or we are not trained to see these hidden elements, we would not appreciate the coat's beauty and would dismiss it as of little interest or value. It does not require much of a stretch of the imagination to appreciate how the concept of *shibui* might apply to the behavior of people we meet in our daily lives.

Students should also take into account the idea that the relationship between husband and wife and between parent and child is not the same as that between teacher and student. A wife does not think of her marriage primarily as a chance to learn from her husband. To avoid, especially in our egalitarian society, the acceptance of a possible subservient or inferior role implied by her recognition of her husband's teacherly accomplishments or development, she may regard them as of little value or even denigrate them. (These comments apply, perhaps to an even greater degree, to the husband whose wife teaches the kind of subject under discussion.) Children must mature and must come to their own conclusions concerning what things are about. They may need to reject their parents' ideas to be able to formulate their own, even if after this process they find themselves in basic agreement with the ideas they had earlier opposed.

Another factor to consider is that a teacher draws only a small fraction of the millions of people who could conceivably come for instruction. Usually these students are attracted to and remain with their teacher because they are basically of the same mind or are traveling similar life paths. The teacher's wife or children probably have not chosen their roles or relationship with him for the same reasons as did his students. For the former he does not function as a teacher, and even if he has been granted some measure of enlightenment, members of his family will be unpredictable in their reaction to such development.

If they become aware of it, the teacher's wife and children often resent the students' scrutiny. Family members may notice that some students seem bent on trying to get to know them better and wonder about their motives. Sometimes they will dismiss students as rather sorry specimens, because the students come to the teacher for instruction. This is more likely to be the case where a teacher's family fails to share the teacher's view of the world.

All these factors make attempts at determining the kind of person a teacher is by observing his family rather unproductive. It is probably natural for students to be curious about their teacher: lifestyle, the kind of spouse chosen, and the kinds of children raised. But attempts at assessment and conclusions drawn are usually reflective of the students' level of development and outlook, and are really ultimately irrelevant. Students will make faster progress if they forgo such attempts in favor of concentrating fully on their practice.

It is the extremely rare teacher who might be considered fully developed in the sense of being all-wise and all-knowing. It is an open question whether such a human being even exists or, for that matter, has ever existed, except in the quite probably distorted thinking of his followers. The teachers I have known have been further along the road students wished to travel, could point the way, and had reached understandings and insights that could dispel some of the illusions to which most of us are subject. But these teachers were still human beings who made mistakes and demonstrated the faults and inconsistencies characteristic of us all.

We should not, therefore, be too surprised when a teacher seems to show a preference for the behavior or even the personality of one student over that of another. We might expect an enlightened teacher to treat each student in the same way, because the teacher knows that students need not accomplish anything, are all right as they are, and can just simply be. Nevertheless, a teacher may still prefer a student who works willingly and diligently to one who seems to lack motivation. He may prefer a good-natured student over a grumpy one and one who bears necessary pain stoically over one who does not.

Even if the teacher is able to avoid showing his personal preference for one student over another, the issue is complicated by the fact that students require individual treatment. Some need to be pushed a bit and others restrained from overdoing. Some require a sympathetic and understanding listener who might suggest viable alternative courses of action, while others must be kept at arm's length, because they want someone to tell them what to do and must be encouraged to come to their own decisions and take responsibility for them and for consequent action. The evenhandedness in the treatment of students we might expect from a good teacher would, then, come in the form of the teacher's effort to do what is necessary to help each student to develop. Thus, students should not expect to be treated alike.

What about a teacher's interaction with students of the opposite sex? The teacher may be sexually attracted to a student and the student to the teacher. Students may view a sexual connection with the teacher as a chance to know the teacher better and perhaps to learn the "secrets" of the art they are studying. The teacher may be flattered by a student's interest and perhaps enjoy the excitement of a romantic liaison. Sexual attraction and union is usually not simply of a gross sensual nature but combines the physical with mental and emotional elements to produce one of the most gratifying experiences we can have. But in the dojo, the interaction between teacher and student necessary for the student's development must take precedence over the more normal male-female interplay. Failure to establish and hold to this priority will, in most cases, slow a student's development or halt it altogether. A fairly obvious reason for this slowing is that the student will view the teacher more as a lover than as a teacher. The two functions have, in our literature, often been happily combined, but in this instance the more important teaching aspect cannot but suffer a decline.

A teacher's special connection with a student is usually sensed by the rest of the school. Often the other students resent the relationship, because the student in question is thought to be getting preferred treatment. Many of the other students may well feel angry, envious, or jealous. Thus, the existence of a teacher-student romance can adversely influence instruction, especially where the teacher professes to be offering students entrance to an esoteric spiritual discipline that students (probably wrongly) perceive as needing to be untainted by more mundane pursuits.

This adverse effect is compounded when a teacher has more than one romance in progress at the same time. When an involved student learns that he or she is not the only recipient of the teacher's affections, the repercussions can be explosive. Such behavior on the part of the teacher and the directly affected students can lead to the disillusionment and exodus of large numbers of students from a school.

To change the subject slightly, socializing with students may make it difficult for a teacher to treat them in the strict and generally impartial way teaching requires. Students are sometimes offended when a teacher's uncompromising attitude toward them in the dojo seems at odds with the friendlier and more relaxed exchange they may enjoy socially.

It is also sometimes difficult for teachers to treat their students as they might other people in matters concerned with everyday life. For example, when students worked for me and received payment, I found myself intolerant of lapses in reliability, dependability, and industriousness. I thought the training they were doing would enhance and strengthen their ability to throw themselves fully into a project they had agreed to undertake. Such hoped-for results were not always evident.

A few students who became tenants in a house I owned were quickly and firmly corrected when they failed to fulfill their obligations in garbage disposal and cleanliness, or otherwise acted to disturb the cooperative atmosphere in the house. I didn't relate to them as I did to other tenants but as students whose development could be enhanced by receiving correction. They seldom welcomed such criticism. Of course, I acted in the belief that our training was really preparation for living our daily life and was not to be thought of as something separate.

The foregoing problems and uncomfortable situations that can occur to disturb the student-teacher relationship are best avoided. Their occurrence is usually of less concern in schools that consider instruction to encompass mainly developing students' fighting skills and their physical strength. But where mental and spiritual training are stressed, these problems are of greater moment and everyone concerned has a big stake in avoiding them.

An optimistic explanation for their appearance might be that both the students involved and the teacher must learn certain lessons from them. Even those students at some remove from the working out and final resolution of a problem are given a chance to experience the situation. Of course, few students will view a disturbing occurrence from this perspective, and most will believe they have to decide whether or not their training has been irreparably damaged and whether or not to move on. They should keep in mind, however, that sometimes an apparent crisis, when fittingly resolved or viewed from a new perspective, can strengthen the desire to get on with training. Working on themselves is, after all, the students' primary reason for being in the *dojo*.

CHAPTER VI

Interaction Among Students

Man is made by his belief. As he believes, so he is.
BHAGAVAD-GITA

STUDENTS ENROLL IN martial arts schools for many reasons. But they stay only a few months unless they find an atmosphere in which they feel comfortable or in which they believe they can develop. Usually the teacher sets the tone in a school and, as stated earlier, a student is drawn to and remains with a teacher because the two are to a great extent of like mind. If the students who remain with a teacher have an affinity for their teacher's view of life, they have this in common with one another as well. Where this shared view includes a desire for noncompetitive training and for helping one another to develop, it would seem that everyone would get on well together. But perhaps because students may also hold other attitudes, or are attached to aberrations they may or may not be trying to correct, students do not always get along well with one another.

In schools of martial arts that stress competitiveness and prepare their students for tournaments, we might expect students to be more at odds with each other, perhaps disliking or seeking to gain some advantage over one another. Surprisingly, I have not found this to be true. Of course, at many of the schools where a sportive martial art is taught, a strong ethical code also prevails. Students are taught to respect their opponents, to play fairly and by the rules, and to win and lose gracefully.

In tournament-oriented schools, students usually practice their techniques in free play or sparring against opponents who do their best to fight back—to resist the technique and to counter with one of their own. But attacks and counterattacks must remain within the bounds set by the rules of the art. For example, in karate, certain areas of the body are off limits as targets for punches and kicks, and moves such as eye or throat poking and throat or testicle grabbing and squeezing are prohibited. Sport judo, too, has strict rules as to what is permitted in throwing and in mat work. But within these bounds players apply and combine their techniques with rather wide latitude in the use of strength, speed, and inventiveness. Naturally, the more experienced players, whose techniques and general skills are well developed, are usually easily able to defeat the relatively inexperienced, who rely mainly on their basic capabilities. In these exchanges between two people who are usually doing their utmost, using whatever skills and physical attributes they have to overcome one another, each becomes quite clear about the other's competence. If players are thrown or must submit to a choke or joint lock in judo, they know what happened. In karate, too, players have little doubt about the ability of their opponent as compared with their own.

More important, in this hard practice students are afforded an unparalleled chance to get to know more about their opponents than technical accomplishments or physical attributes. An opponent's character is easily discerned through martial arts practice, and what we learn about that person's true nature does not always square with the way he or she tries to appear to others. For example, a person may wish to seem easygoing and accommodating, but in action displays unwarranted stubborn resistance, aggressiveness, and hostility. In this rather revealing training environment, students who refuse to give the practice their best, who have tendencies that border on the sadistic, or who play unfairly stay only a short time. As beginners they encounter an overwhelmingly superior force inimical to their attitude—in the form of their teacher and senior students, from whom they cannot hide and whose skill they cannot match. The result of this weeding-out process is that the students who remain usually share a similar outlook. Common to this outlook are such characteristics as a willingness to work hard, a reluctance to take unfair advantage of others, and perseverance despite difficult or overwhelming odds, to name just a few. Among these students grows a camaraderie based on a realistic assessment of one another's ability.

This process in schools or clubs of martial arts that are sport-oriented can be enhanced by the teacher's attempts to get students to see the limitations and the negative aspects of competition. If a teacher is aware of such negative aspects, we might wonder why he allows his students to take part in tournaments at all. Unfortunately, the teacher and his martial art are usually connected to a whole network of other teachers and schools, sometimes constituting a worldwide system. Teachers have usually been nurtured in this system and are bound by duties and obligations both to those of higher rank and to the art itself. For a teacher to break with all this and to go his own way is difficult.

It is possible to rationalize competition in a number of ways. Some martial arts teachers hold tournaments to give their students a chance to observe their functioning under more stressful conditions than they encounter in the *dojo*. We might embrace the view that engaging in an activity, actually experiencing it, can be of value in coming to understand its uselessness or harmfulness. Thus, competition gives us a chance to see that winning and losing are ultimately the same. Also, if we must function in a competitive environment, we can learn to maintain our mental equilibrium by developing a large measure of detachment both from the actual competition and from its outcome.

All of the foregoing ideas, as well as many others to do with self-development and self-understanding, abound in schools where students do not compete. In fact, by contrast with the sport-oriented schools, at the noncompetitive ones we often hear a great deal more talking about self-realization and about spirituality. The workout or practice at these schools is much more controlled than in sportive schools. The emphasis is on making physical movement accord with philosophical principles. Students are told to use a minimum of strength in their movements, to give up resistance, and to move from the *tan tien* or *tanden*. For months and years this emphasis might be said to inhibit students' actions, and some feel that they cannot let themselves go or do their utmost against their opponent. Though beginners may intellectually appreciate the value of a noncompetitive approach, they may not have internalized it and at heart are still quite concerned with winning and losing. Nor are they yet able to hold their own by using the yielding, highly sensitive method of dealing with an opponent their teacher advocates. The frustration consequently engendered is useful in helping students to recognize and to let go of their conditioned ideas, but it is frustration nonetheless.

People attracted to this kind of martial art, or to a martial art taught in this way, will be different from those drawn to the sportive schools. Sometimes the former will exhibit a fair measure of arrogance or sense of superiority based on their belief that they are on to an esoteric something that will give them certain powers and, they hope, change their lives for the better. Even though their training may be difficult, they are not subject to the sometimes harsh and humbling reality beginners face in a sportive school. Consequently, they may be able to retain for a longer period certain unproductive attitudes with their fellow students, which the more incandescent environment of rough-and-tumble practice usually burns away. Moreover, they are not afforded the release that hard physical effort gives members of the sportive schools. All these factors may account for what I have found to be a relatively colder, less friendly, and more self-preoccupied attitude in nonsportive schools of martial arts.

Clearly, my comments are generalizations. Some sportive schools may exhibit the characteristics I sense in the nonsportive ones. Usually, too, teachers bear a great portion of the responsibility for their school's atmosphere and its effect on students, so that it is not just a matter of what is taught, or even how, but of the quality and degree of the teacher's development.

Whatever the school's atmosphere, students will feel drawn to one another for various reasons, ranging from the shared experience of enrolling together as beginners to the pull of sexual attraction. A number will get together to have something to eat or to drink after practice, and some may pair off. Rejection or nonacceptance of fellow students may play its part where senior students, who have been studying for a number of years, may band together and only reluctantly and selectively welcome newer students. If a ranking system operates, the higher belts might only admit to their group students who have been promoted to a certain level and have proved themselves. Sometimes those of higher rank may display arrogance and a swaggering manner, a deplorable development and one that the teacher should have noticed and eliminated. But if the teacher and the students are too caught up in the competitive aspects of their martial art, the successful competitors may well develop mentally and spiritually in a less than satisfactory way. Such a situation will also have negative consequences for junior students.

To turn the discussion to the behavior of individual students with one another, students may find themselves in a situation in which a fellow student does not appear to be following the teacher's suggestions. This usually occurs when a student relies too much on strength instead of technique or resists when the teaching emphasizes nonresistance. It is also likely that in the early years of training such tactics may enable the physically stronger student to overcome the weaker. The weaker then may be tempted to criticize the stronger's efforts, ostensibly to attempt to help and to correct the stronger. But the criticism may spring from less laudatory motives, like frustration and anger stemming from the physically weaker student's inability to cope successfully with the stronger's tactics. It may be a way of carrying a counterattack from the mat or floor to the verbal arena, where the weaker student may feel less disadvantaged.

Criticism of this nature is best avoided. We may be mistaken in thinking that fellow students are willfully doing something we believe improper. Those students may be following the prescribed method as closely as they can, given their mental and physical capabilities. They may be well aware of their inadequacies and may be working hard to correct them. Unless a fellow student asks for our advice or help, we should continue to work on perfecting the many weaknesses in our own technique or filling gaps in our understanding. It is likely that we will exert a more positive influence on fellow students if we demonstrate rather than merely verbally express a technique or a way of moving.

Ultimately we derive greater benefit from considering success or failure in attack and defense as of secondary importance. The primary concern is simply following as best we can the principles undergirding our art. Proceeding on this basis will not only allow our martial arts ability optimum growth but will enhance our development on other levels as well.

The foregoing is not to say we should have no interest in helping fellow students improve their technique. Depending on students' readiness and receptivity, we can certainly suggest improvements in such areas as hand or foot placement, body movement, or timing. But when making suggestions we should try to be as clear as we can about our motives. We should avoid attempting through our recommendations to establish psychological superiority. And we should be careful that our suggestions don't make our training partner timid out of a feeling of gratefulness, deference, or an overly self-conscious attempt to make a move correctly.

A senior student would do well to refrain from correcting a junior's mistakes, if the senior cannot easily demonstrate the superiority of his method over the junior's. If a junior, through his greater strength or other innate ability, can frustrate the senior's techniques, the junior may be reluctant to accept advice or correction. This is especially so if the value of the correction requires months or years to become apparent. It is unfortunate that the junior's superior strength, speed, or coordination may then actually become detrimental or serve as a handicap to his future development. If he thinks he can already handle senior students, he may be reluctant to do the patient work of building the foundation required for continuing progress in his art.

Sometimes one student will dislike another. The two may try to avoid practicing with one another, but given the general changing-about in sparring practice or in free play, they will encounter one another periodically. The teacher should be alert to any displays of anger or attempts to hurt one another when these two antagonistic students practice together. They could be kept apart, but separation would not facilitate their recognizing and perhaps even releasing a point of view that makes them unable to get along together. In the often heated exchanges characteristic of hard practice, they are given a chance to learn to understand or at least to tolerate one another.

In my own judo and karate training in Hawaii and in Japan I sometimes encountered antiwhite and antiforeign prejudice on the part of a few fellow students. I never confronted these attitudes directly but attempted through working hard at my training to demonstrate my seriousness and to become competent enough to rank as a strong adversary. Although competence and even superiority in the art we were studying did not always serve to erase prejudice, in most cases it earned a grudging respect. One might have hoped that the training we were all undergoing would overcome such negative feelings of prejudice of one sort or another, but unfortunately this was not always true.

48

Another disturbing situation in the practice hall arises when one student likes another too much. This usually occurs in schools where men and women practice together. Interaction can be of a somewhat intimate nature where practice partners stand physically close and must hold or touch one another. Obviously, opportunities are afforded for one student, almost always a man, to take liberties with his woman partner. If the woman resents this intrusion, she may suffer in silence or may speak to the offender, or to the teacher, about the problem. The teacher is well advised to handle this subject somewhat carefully, whether he notices it himself or is informed of it, because it is potentially embarrassing to those involved. The man may deny any wrongdoing and claim the woman imagined it. On the other hand, he may admit it and say that she welcomed the attention. Usually, in such a situation the woman finds herself in an increasingly uncomfortable position. The general scenario appears in various forms in today's society wherever men and women work or play together. But if we regard our *dojo* as a special place in which we have an opportunity to work on perfecting ourselves, we should control tendencies that could make such work more difficult.

We cannot forget, however, that people are attracted to one another, whether the attraction is physical, mental, spiritual, or a combination of the three. If we become interested in another student, we would do well to pursue this interest outside the training hall, while we try to maintain proper decorum and discretion in training. As our success in focusing our minds on our training increases, we will be less likely to become disturbed by other attractions.

Finally, the best prescription I can think of to avoid most of the problems I have presented is for students to consider their fellow students as brothers and sisters. It is true that siblings do not always get on well together and that rivalry and even incest are not unusual. But observed in the best sense, a brotherly and sisterly feeling for our fellow students would make us go out of our way to understand and tolerate their imperfections, to care for them, and to help them to develop.

Unfortunately, despite the teacher's attempts to persuade students of the usefulness of such an approach, some students will be unable to embrace it or come to a sadly deficient interpretation of it. The best we can do in relating to such students is to hold to our convictions—even though these individuals may not feel or act toward us as we toward them—and to continue to work on ourselves. There is a good chance that as we develop, the changes in us will affect in a positive way those with whom we interact.

CHAPTER VII

Actions and Attitudes That Hinder Development

> In the pursuit of learning one knows more every day; in the pursuit of the way one does less every day. One does less and less until one does nothing at all, and when one does nothing at all there is nothing that is undone.
>
> LAO TZU

As THE YEARS go by and we continue to practice, we may look for opportunities outside the dojo to broaden and deepen our knowledge of martial arts. Unfortunately, these hopes are seldom realized and such activities may even prove a hindrance. For instance, we may decide to visit another school of martial arts, usually one teaching the same art as ours. The reason we will give for visiting will be curiosity, a desire to see what other students are doing, so that we can add breadth to our training and increase our knowledge. On the surface it might seem that curiosity of this sort is laudable and should be encouraged. But as we look deeper we might notice that going elsewhere to see what is happening there might indicate a certain restlessness and a belief that our training lacks something. An extreme expression of our unsettledness and doubt might extend to our enrollment in another school, while we continue to attend our own, in the hope of making faster progress.

Even if we want nothing more from our practice than to learn a useful skill, we would be well advised to remain quietly with one teacher for perhaps five years, learning what that teacher has to impart. Learning just one throw in judo so that we can successfully use it against strong and

53

determined resistance takes a minimum of three to four years of three-day-a-week practice sessions. This is because we must work to establish certain mental and physical patterns until we have formed a kind of conditioned reflex. We will gain little additional expertise and may even lose some of what we have by attempting to alter the physical and mental patterns we have already established. Furthermore, if our two teachers differ in their way of performing a particular technique, and they usually will, we will find ourselves somewhat confused and upset as we try to resolve the differences. If we choose one teacher's approach to the technique, how do we explain or justify our method when we are practicing at the other teacher's school? A teacher is usually not pleased to know that one of his beginners is attending another teacher's classes. The displeasure is not caused just by a bruised ego but also by the knowledge that the student's early training almost always suffers in this situation.

Another problem with learning from two teachers at the same time is that the student will probably make comparisons between the two, both in their grasp of and ability to teach technique, and if his interest extends to it, in their mental and spiritual development. Of course, he may not go to the extreme of trying in class to contradict one teacher's pronouncements with those made by another. But comparison and the accompanying judgment, even if only in the student's mind, usually cause conflict, confusion, and suffering. Each teacher is what he is, and we should accept him on that basis rather than focusing on what appear to be faults or deficiencies. Moreover, the student, in his early years of training, usually does not know enough to determine what a teacher's strengths and weaknesses are.

If our martial art is sportive, we may visit another school to look over or scout players we expect to encounter in an approaching tournament. But to see players in action does not contribute much to our ability to cope with their techniques. Practicing with them, actually experiencing their way of moving, would give us more of a chance of assessing their capabilities. Without this practice, merely watching a player's moves will not go very far in helping us form an assessment, except in rather general terms. Therefore, success in sportive martial arts is most likely to be achieved by working hard on our own techniques with our fellow students. As we improve, those we train with will also improve through their attempts to devise methods of coping with our attack or defense. Persistence and diligence in practice, without thought of potential opponents, can produce a competitor whose abilities will be equal to most tests.

Where martial arts training seeks to internalize certain realizations or insights, there seems even less reason, in our early years, to visit another school. Our teacher will have set down general principles and methods that we can use to work on ourselves, a process requiring effort over many years and usually a lifetime. To go elsewhere, to hear and to entertain conflicting ideas, is a kind of indulgence and can get in the way of our development. It may also indicate a lack of seriousness about our efforts and should alert us to the possibililty that we are becoming less involved with or dedicated to what we are doing. Doubts about the ultimate value of what we are attempting to learn or about the method we have chosen should have been resolved at the outset. In time our training will prove useful and productive, but we must be willing to suspend judgment for a few years or we will add additional hurdles to the course, some of them perhaps insurmountable.

My own early training, which began in Hawaii in judo classes taught at the Nuuanu YMCA by Yamamoto Yukiso, combined sportiveness with a somewhat muted Japanese samurai warrior philosphy. In Hawaii, going elsewhere for instruction when already enrolled in a school was considered disloyal and was almost unheard of. In the late forties tournaments were held rather infrequently and practice was not geared to preparing for outside competition. It was, however, directed toward technique development and perfection, and was physically and mentally demanding. Because Yamamoto was an excellent teacher, many of us who entered tournaments did well. Concentration on our own practice, unaffected by outside influences, enabled a number of us to develop techniques that the students of other schools found difficult to resist. I believe this grounding of a number of years of consistent and steady training with one instructor lays the kind of solid foundation which can eventually allow us to benefit from another teacher's instruction or to proceed on our own, if we wish to do so.

When, however, in our early years of training, should we leave our teacher and go elsewhere? We should look for other instruction if we are asked to behave in a manner that feels wrong or seems overly dangerous. For example, we may dislike the seeming brutality or excessive physicality our training appears to require. Perhaps we detect mental or emotional imbalances in our teacher that seem to have nothing to do with the self-realization of either of us. However, in such cases, it is really in our interest to give long and careful consideration to the possibility that our decision to leave is based primarily on our reluctance to give up our accustomed but deluded way of thinking and acting. When we sense a questioning of or an attack on our way of seeing and dealing with the world, we become defensive and may be disinclined to make changes or to suffer further buffetings. We must realize that the process we are engaged in will, at times, include a measure of pain and discomfort as we push beyond previous physical and mental limitations. Furthermore, confidence in our teacher's methods should come from our having chosen carefully at the outset.

To elaborate a bit more on the material on choosing a teacher presented in my earlier book, *The Martial Spirit*, we may feel that our best chance for receiving authentic instruction will come if we enroll at a school taught by a person raised in the culture that developed the martial art. Because in the past the skill and technique of Asian martial artists have been superior to that of non-Asians, people interested in a sportive martial art have usually looked for an Asian teacher. But the picture has changed somewhat, in that the skill of the non-Asians has, in recent years, reached world-class levels. Thus, those interested in studying a sportive martial art need not confine their search to Asian teachers but might find instruction of superior quality among non-Asians.

If we seek something more than sport from a martial art, we may find that choosing a teacher poses greater difficulties. Our reading may have led us to believe that another culture has reached deeper understandings than has ours about man's place in the world or emphasizes spiritual values in life to a greater degree that does ours. In an effort to share or grasp these insights, we may look for a teacher from that culture, reasoning that the foreign culture and the teacher will reflect and embody the insights we seek. Also, we will probably think that the teacher's point of view, what he teaches, how he teaches it, and all the attached ritualistic ways of behaving must be accepted fully and observed to the letter. It probably will do us little harm to religiously accept and observe all we are presented with in our first few years of training. But our training and other influences on our mind will eventually allow us to make a distinction between the form of what we are doing and its substance. We may begin to notice that we are confusing cultural conditioning, or behavior peculiar to a culture, with the essential elements of training. The two do not necessarily go together. Nor should we lose sight of the fact that what we seek is to break through conditioning to that understanding of life that is fundamental to all mankind.

We must remember, also, that the training we have chosen to undertake may not have been the only, or even the most important, influence on the folkways and behavior of people in the culture from which the training derives. For example, if we study a martial art that is steeped in Zen Buddhism and taught by a Japanese, we may believe that we are getting the essence of Japanese culture and that our teacher has developed mainly through his Zen training. Gaining an understanding of Zen and determining what its effect on a culture or a person actually is are difficult enough. But some students of Japanese culture maintain that over the centuries it has been more strongly affected by Shintoism and Confucianism than by Buddhism. Buddhism itself comprises a number of sects with varied beliefs and is not simply Zen. Nor can we ignore the nineteenth- and twentieth-century impact of the West on Japanese thinking and behavior. Thus, our teacher's behavior and attitude probably contain a generous measure of cultural impress, some of which may be extraneous, or even an impediment, to our training.

As we continue to practice, we should achieve greater clarity about the relevance to our development of the various aspects of our training. Moreover, this training should cultivate in us a certain detachment from whatever we do, and this includes the training itself. That is, we must not mistake the training for the realizations we seek. Our teacher must be seen as a guide who can point the way, not as an infallible person whom we can lean upon and without whom we would feel lost. When we grasp these truths and have achieved many of the results practicing can provide, we might well continue training. But we will do so because we believe that it is an important part of our life and that we train because we enjoy it.

Another aspect of martial arts that may retard students' development is the use of a ranking system. Many martial arts rank their students and teachers. A martial art will, of course, reflect the culture in which it originated and that culture the thinking and feeling of its people. Thus, a culture that is hierarchical, one in which people are comfortable when they know their place in society, as well as the relative place of anyone they are likely encounter, will fit into this hierarchical mold anything it originates or touches. Our society, although not the same as the Asian societies from which we borrowed martial arts, seems more comfortable with ranking than without. This may have to do with our competitiveness and our desire to make measurable and quantifiable progress in some direction. In sports, we usually judge the superiority of one individual or team over another on the basis of which scores higher. We rate success in life primarily by the amount of money we earn or have accumulated or, less often, by the position we have achieved.

It is true that a ranking system, fairly administered, has its uses. The rank of teachers, especially, gives prospective students some indication of their skill, knowledge, and experience. Students, too, seem to like to measure their progress by their rise on the promotional ladder. Where students must compete, a ranking system ensures that they are not over- or undermatched.

Rank does not, however, always function as a reliable indicator of a teacher's competence or development, because some teachers promote themselves to higher degrees without the approval of a larger group of senior martial artists. Also, where such a senior group exists, promotions are sometimes awarded those who are politically astute, who function as part of the group's controlling element, or who play the "game" in approved fashion. Nevertheless, in my experience, increased technical competence usually accompanies an advanced degree, even if other aspects of a teacher's development may fail to reflect this rank.

If we are, however, concerned with mental and spiritual growth as much as we are with acquiring skill, we might question the value of a grading

58

and ranking system. How does such a system affect us? Too often we become caught up in thinking about making the next grade or in promotion to black belt, believing that when we reach our goal we will be transformed in some way. It occurs to few of us that the way we function in our American society, our desire for visible exterior indicators of achievement, and our goal-oriented, ambitious approach to whatever we do are all transferred to the *dojo*. Thus, instead of helping us to break the hold on our mind of our conditioning, our training supports it.

The ranking of students is also clearly connected to competition. If we promote, given sufficient time in grade, largely on the basis of tournament wins, aspiring students will naturally try to prepare themselves to do well in tournaments. But their hard work will be done for the wrong reasons and will affect them adversely. Competition tends to make us hard and ruthless, intent on overcoming those who are after the same prize as we, reinforcing ideas of our separateness rather than our connectedness. Concerns centering on achieving self-realization often are relegated to insignificance in this environment.

My experience with formal competition was, in the main, with judo. I lost few matches during my career, and none during the first four or five years, becoming the all-weights Hawaiian Territorial champion for two years in the early 1950s. After winning for a time, I found that I had a big psychological stake in continuing to win. As a consequence, a few days before an impending match I suffered from anxiety and nervousness. I did not attempt to determine the underlying reasons for these feelings. I thought my discomfort was only natural, because I knew that many athletes experienced "butterflies" before races or games and that most of us have some of these symptoms before undergoing a test of some sort. I remain unsure of all of the causes of my anxiety, but certain obvious ones certainly come to mind. Chief among them was an unwillingness to give up the image I had of myself as among the top judomen in the area—if not the top judoman. After a victory, I enjoyed a period of freedom from anxiety and a sense of accomplishment. But this was of relatively short duration and I soon returned to worrying about the progress of possible challengers and about approaching tournaments.

My training suffered from these conditions, though on the surface it may have appeared that I was practicing hard and was making excellent progress. My diligence had more to do with my desire to keep ahead of my competitors than with developing myself in various ways. Losing one or more matches would have undermined my self-image and deflated my ego. Thus defeat might well have been healthful—but I did not want to suffer the accompanying pain. It was not until after leaving the competitive environment that I reached certain insights allowing me to transcend my concern with victory and defeat. Perhaps enduring a longer period of competition might have effected salutary changes, but the eight years of my involvement failed to do so.

Those competitors who are generally successful in tournaments may be unwilling to give up competing, because they depend on their wins for ego gratification or for helping them to establish their identity. Without the periodic ego reinforcement of successful martial arts competition, they may feel lost. This is especially so when they sense, or imagine they sense, that their companions and friends expect a periodic demonstration of their strength and power.

Our years of competitive success may cause a friend or loved one to take our winning for granted, reacting with disbelief and disappointment when we lose. If our martial arts ability and our success in this field constitute a large part of our attractiveness, our relationship may well weaken. In such a case, not only will we suffer from the additional stress and pressure caused by our wish to meet another's expectations, but as long as we try to conform to the fantasy another has of us, we will be less likely to transcend a shallow and limited view of our training.

In summary, competition to determine the superiority, or the ascendancy, of one person, school, or system over another seems flawed if our aim in training is to break through our illusions, to become enlightened, to see reality more clearly—or whatever terms are used to express our attempts at self-realization. In our extremely competitive society, it should cause no surprise when our activities, including martial arts training, display a large measure of competition. But our recognition of the detrimental effects of competition may influence us to try to avoid it and we may gravitate toward a martial art in which competition is absent or held to a minimum. It is interesting to note that in the early days of Kano Jigoro's judo, competition was held infrequently and thought of primarily as a way for students to view their performance under the added stress of a competitive situation. It is not difficult to see that competitors' bearing under stress has more to do with the extent to which they have internalized mental and spiritual values than with their mastery of technique or even their success in previous matches.

In this and earlier chapters I have made more than one reference to the physical and mental pain we sometimes feel when we practice martial arts. Physical pain results when we overtax our body in training or incur some injury. Mental pain can come when we undertake the difficult work of changing mistaken, shallow, or narrow beliefs or ideas, which nevertheless are comfortable, for others closer to reality.

My martial arts career has seen not only a number of badly sprained ankles but broken and sprained toes and fingers, torn knee cartilage and ligaments, a shoulder separation, and hyperextended elbow joints. More than once over the years I wondered why I subjected my body to this unkind treatment. Other than the fact that I enjoyed this training, the rather obvious answer was that the result in strength, skill, and mental and spiritual development was worth the price. Moreover, I never felt particularly upset after suffering an injury, thinking it regrettable but a part of the game.

I have read theories that seek to account for people having accidents or sustaining injuries of the kind I describe by citing the probable presence of underlying emotional problems. Some psychiatrists hold that injury-prone people are often the children of authoritarian parents. When these children grow up, they seem to have difficulty relating to authority. They may seek injury to gain sympathy, to provide an excuse for failing to meet certain standards, or for any number of other reasons. The problem, however, is said to stem from an emotional difficulty that the psychiatrist eventually unearths, treats, and cures.

My parents certainly were authoritarian and I know that I rebelled against their dictates. Moreover, I recognize in myself a reluctance to obey orders blindly or to follow a policy I judge ill-conceived, no matter what its source. Such an attitude probably comes under the heading of having difficulty with authority. I realize also that I have arranged my life in such a way that I have little direct contact with anyone in a position to control my thinking and actions. Of course, I am aware of how all of our lives are controlled to some extent by governmental and economic interests. Social constraints also keep the actions of all of us within certain bounds. But I refer more specifically to my avoidance of jobs in which I have to tailor my outlook or actions to the expectations of someone in a higher position. My study of martial arts may have suffered slightly from this attitude, because although I was willing to place myself in the hands of a person I respected and from whom I felt I could learn, his teachings had to make sense eventually. Thus, I did not follow unquestioningly and regarded my teachers as fallible human beings rather than as persons who possessed a secret power that somehow made them almost superhuman.

Does such behavior stem from underlying emotional problems? I doubt it. Practicing martial arts certainly placed me in a position in which I had to give and receive physical punishment. I know that in my earlier years I needed an outlet for the anger and frustration I felt when the elements that constituted my life failed to form the patterns I thought they should. Martial arts provided a physical release for those feelings and kept them at reasonable levels. But this release did not come from hurting others or being hurt myself. Rather, it seemed to come through expending the energy generated by anger or whatever factors were responsible for producing my mental and physical tension. After a hard practice session I was physically spent and, apparently as a consequence, felt both physically and mentally relaxed.

Nevertheless, martial arts certainly have their violent aspects and attract some people who wish to inflict pain on, and perhaps destroy, others and themselves. I have been struck with the unusually high number of violent accidental deaths of young martial artists who were my students or whom I knew personally. One was killed in a parachute jump, one in a small plane crash, another through complications of an injury suffered in practice, still another in a motorcycle crash, and two from falls in mountainous country. Another two died prematurely from illness (one in his early forties and the other in his mid-fifties). This relatively large number of early and violent deaths among martial artists with whom I was acquainted certainly opens the door to speculation concerning a "death wish."

62

Martial artists who want to hurt not themselves but their practice partners are, in my experience, quite rare. As I remarked earlier, teachers and senior students strongly discourage such behavior in beginners. Beginning students with sadistic tendencies invariably leave after a few months of training, much before they have gained enough expertise to become dangerous. Fighting and hurting people outside the *dojo*, also, are inveighed against and usually result in expulsion.

Regarding mental pain, we might suffer it when we become aware of tendencies in ourselves that fail to accord with an idealized self-image. Doing poorly with an opponent may upset us, especially when our expectations of victory are high and we have not yet learned to be altogether without expectations, or gotten to the point where winning and losing are borne with equanimity. We may think we have transcended feelings of resentment, anger or hostility when confronted with an aggressive opponent, only to find these emotions rising in us. The appearance of these negative feelings may disappoint and depress us. Finally, fear of suffering an incapacitating injury may become an unwelcome preoccupation, inhibiting the spontaneity of our functioning both in the *dojo* and in everyday life.

We may feel these examples of mental pain, as well as many I have not mentioned, even more intensely than we feel physical pain. But our suffering should not deter us from continuing with our training, because the training offers a way of letting go of the mistaken views and beliefs that often cause our distress.

Because controlled violence forms the foundation of martial arts, this training can bring us both physical and mental pain. For the large majority, however, the benefits of practice far outweigh the pain. Moreover, sustaining an injury, whether physical or mental, invariably springs from deeper-rooted causes than the simple one of our having had "an accident." Such an incident can help us develop greater insight into how our minds function. Through becoming aware of our thinking and feeling, and of events preceding an injury, we can determine for ourselves if psychological theories concerned with injury-prone individuals are valid for us or not. Again, if such theories or others are revelant, our training can help us discover and deal with the underlying causes.

Finally, one additional area students might well shun is martial arts politics. Engaging in politics is a temptation not so much for students as it is for higher-ranking players who are usually also teachers. By "politics" I mean holding office or becoming active in an organization that administers or controls schools or clubs of martial arts by formulating rules and procedures concerned with students' ranking and grading, and deciding standards that schools must meet for group membership. Politics may attract us because we wish to wield power. But the various methods we originate and use to exercise and keep control are of the sort that reinforce the limiting aspects of our culture that our training is designed to help us to perceive and to transcend. Thus, if we use our connection with martial arts to pursue politics, we will expend our limited energies on endeavors that will do little to further, and may well block, our development, to say nothing of the adverse effect our example may have on those whom we teach.

Our motives for politicking may seem quite altruistic and laudable, such as attempting to improve the quality of teaching in our art or to institute various reforms. A Taoist view of such attempts, however, would be that trying to tamper with the current state of affairs could well worsen them. We can never accurately predict all the results of our actions. Aggressive efforts at reform or improvement may have an unwanted effect on areas or levels that completely escaped our notice.

Of course, we can learn from everything we do. Engaging in political activities, or spending our time in some of the other nonproductive ways I have suggested, may help us to see that we have taken a wrong turning. But it is unnecessary to suffer through every possible mistake we are capable of making when some foresight, intuitive sense, or advice from a more experienced person who has covered the ground may help us hold to a more fruitful course.

We cannot avoid making some mistakes and should not fear doing so. Youthful energy and attendant strong drives will push us or attract us to actions or ways of behaving that a diminishing of this energy (or perhaps experience and wisdom) might reveal to be extreme, unbalanced, or otherwise undesirable. We will then have to do what we can to extricate ourselves from our predicament or to change what is no longer comfortable. Although we may be unaware of it, this process goes on all the time, with small and continuing changes in us making themselves slowly manifest in our outward actions and behavior. Awareness of all of this usually comes, however, only after we have undergone some appreciable, and seemingly sudden, inward change and feel the pressure to make a corresponding outward change.

CHAPTER VIII

Assessing the Value
of Our Training

> When the best student hears about the way,
> He practices it assiduously;
> When the average student hears about the way,
> It seems to him one moment there and gone the next;
> When the worst student hears about the way,
> He laughs out loud.
> If he did not laugh
> It would be unworthy of being the way.
>
> LAO TZU

OVER THE YEARS I have practiced with, worked with, and been taught by, many high-ranking martial artists. My foregoing suggestions about resisting the temptation to try to determine how martial arts training has molded these men and how it has developed them spiritually by learning how they behaved outside the *dojo,* or how their wives and children acted, derive from my experience and ultimate conclusion that such attempts are of little value for our own development.

When I began my training I was concerned mainly with becoming stronger and more skillful. I admired higher-ranking players because they possessed and exhibited the power and expertise I sought. In addition, as I learned more about the possible effect of training on practitioners' minds and spirits, I expected higher-ranking martial artists to possess a certain tranquil demeanor, to see their development reflected in a special outlook on life or in an exceptional way of living. Unfortunately, I was seldom in a position to see how they lived, because my contact with them was limited to the dojo. Here they functioned in a milieu in which they felt at home, were at or near the top in terms of ability, and were treated with respect and deference. While I was, in general, favorably impressed with the development of these men, it did cross my mind that their behavior might have been different in more difficult or less congenial surroundings.

My experience during my first decade in martial arts (beginning in 1948) encompassed judo training for five years in Hawaii, a year in Chicago, and a year and a half in California, as well as two years of judo and karate in Japan. Toward the end of the 1950s I went to New York City to work and to teach martial arts. There I was given an opportunity to experience the way of thinking and functioning of martial artists outside the dojo. I was at the time third-degree black belt in judo and first-degree in karate. For all sorts of reasons, not the least of which was to profit financially from the public's need for and interest in self-defense, a great number of judo schools had begun to spring up all over the New York area. To attempt to keep judo close to Kodokan ideals, older and higher-ranking players, including myself, soon formed a group concerned with organizing these schools, setting up a controlling body to run tournaments and awarding promotions fairly. This local group became affiliated with a national judo body and with the Kodokan in Japan. We held monthly meetings to thrash out policy and arrive at a direction for judo in our region. I was elected treasurer and later vice-president of this organization. Holding these positions involved me rather heavily in judo politics.

My reactions and feelings about this kind of activity were at first of optimism about the possibility of moving the development of judo in New York in directions I felt were useful and correct or, at least, those I favored. As time went on, however, lines of contention began to form among the members of our group based on what seemed self-interest. Some may think that such an outcome should have come as no surprise, but I had thought, perhaps naively, that judo was valuable as training in self-perfection and should be treated as something special. It seemed that our group dynamics, or whatever goes on among people who get together for a particular purpose, were not particularly changed by the mental and spiritual influences of judo. Our way of dealing with judo and with one another seemed little different from what it would have been if we had studied and practiced some other sport or subject. Of course, an important consideration here is that many of us regarded judo primarily as a sport and did not attach any great additional significance to it.

If our judo training did reveal itself, it could well have been in the tenacity we exhibited in defending our positions and, consequently, in the trouble we experienced in agreeing on most issues. Yet, in retrospect, I realize I witnessed the result not only of judo training, but of this training combined with the egalitarianism and emphasis on individuality of American culture. This combination could produce a strong-minded, contentious individual, unwilling to entertain or accept a point of view at variance with his own. Seemingly, strength and independence of mind must be tempered by a perceptiveness or sensitivity that penetrates the surface of events and is attuned to life's rhythms, lest it lead to stubbornness, short-sightedness and inflexibility.

While in New York in the early sixties, I also attended meetings of a karate group that was engaged in forming an organization of Japan Karate Association (J.K.A.) clubs on the East coast. The group was headed by one of my former karate teachers in Japan who had been invited to come here to teach by a Philadelphia karate club. The members of our karate organization met periodically for promotional examinations. We also held tournaments, but they were infrequent and participants were limited to karate men who had learned the J.K.A. style.

In contrast to the judo organization discussed above, the karate organization functioned more as might a Japanese group, because it was directed and controlled by Japanese who held the higher ranks. The lower-ranking Americans, who were or had been karate students, were accustomed to treating the Japanese with respect and deference. Group discussions concerning any problems usually switched to the Japanese language, because it was easier for the Japanese to express themselves in their native tongue. Moreover, they seemed to proceed as if they could communicate with one another in ways Americans could not and on levels out of our reach. Possibly they thought their karate training had been of a higher standard than ours or that they had somehow absorbed their native martial arts traditions and we understood these traditions only partially or not at all. Their approach, however, also seemed designed, or served, to keep Americans in a subservient position.

The Japanese, in general, justified their actions and attitudes by arguing that the art was theirs and that they were best qualified to administer it without the help of Americans, who differed from them in the way they saw the world. Moreover, the hierarchial Japanese societal arrangement expresses itself in juniors almost always deferring to seniors. Therefore, lower-ranking karate men were not expected to challenge the pronouncements of those above them, but to follow loyally even if they disagreed.

Another way the Japanese were able for a time to control karate and, in earlier days, judo outside of Japan was through the awarding of promotions. The higher-ranking judo and karate teachers had the authority to promote and were able to impede the Americans' rise in the martial arts hierarchy by promoting them slowly. In both judo and karate, promotions took much longer to achieve than in Japan, in an ostensible effort to keep the quality of ranks the same. This practice and its rationale were partly valid, especially in promotions to ranks of third-degree black belt and above, because America had too few top-quality practitioners. A related factor was that the Japanese teachers, who were generally tournament- and competition-oriented, gradually lost some of their sharpness, because the level of ability here offered them insufficient challenge. Where further promotion depended on tournament wins, their removal from such opportunity usually, also, served to slow or halt their rise in rank.

As Americans gained in ability and began to close the gap in skill between themselves and the Japanese, the Japanese continued to promote Americans slowly and tried to maintain the relative difference in rank that obtained at the outset. Holding this difference helped the Japanese in their effort at control and kept lower-ranking Americans subject to following the dictates of the Japanese. Avoiding absolutely any narrowing of the gap in rank was obviously not possible, but ground was given slowly and mainly to those American martial artists who behaved in an approved fashion.

I may seem overly critical of the Japanese attempt to control martial arts in this area. To soften the picture somewhat, I should say that first of all, not all the Japanese who were here to teach martial arts acted in the way I have described. There were mitigating factors, also, in that the individuals in question were young and had not yet developed sufficient

70

insight to allow a longer and broader view. Regarded from the standpoint of achieving and wielding power, those who desire it and come into a position of dominance seem to relinquish, or even to share, their power only with great reluctance. The existence of a ranking system gave those with authority to award promotions a great deal of influence and prestige, because teachers and students all wanted to rise in grade. In most karate and judo circles, one measured achievement and ability by grade level, despite lip service to the contrary. Finally, it is not easy for anyone to make a smooth transition from one culture, or one way of doing things, to another. Few of us can free our minds of our conditioning, and the Japanese in question were in this regard not exceptional.

In any case, whatever the rationale for the Japanese outlook and actions, there was no doubt in my mind that they did everything they could to control the style of karate I taught. Judo in the area had already evolved too far to permit the Japanese involved to exercise control to the degree they might have wished, but the pattern described was not uncharacteristic of local, national, and international judo affairs.

I had yet another chance to view martial arts in a context broader than that of the dojo when I began studying tai chi chuan in the mid-sixties in New York with Cheng Man-ching. I had had no real contact with an internal or soft style of boxing, was impressed with that approach and with Cheng's ability, and began to work to incorporate softer or more yielding principles into the martial arts knowledge I had gained in the preceding twenty years. At the same time, it was interesting and valuable to experience Cheng's teaching and to hear what he had to say. It was also instructive to see Cheng's interaction, and that of our club, with a clannish and sometimes hostile Chinese community.

Cheng came to New York and was invited to teach tai chi by interested Chinese who had heard of his skill in that art. Apparently because they were unable to pay him enough to support his family, and so that he could earn additional income, they agreed to allow him to teach non-Chinese. This was something of a concession, because Chinese in America had in the past been extremely reluctant to instruct non-Chinese in Chinese martial arts. Secretiveness and clannishness have been said to be characteristic of the Cantonese, who constitute the great majority of Chinese immigrants in America. Justification for the Chinese attitude is easily found in the record of our country's shabby and racially prejudiced treatment of Chinese over more than a century. But for non-Chinese who are not familiar with the historical background, as well as for many who are, direct experience of Chinese hostility toward and mistrust of non-Chinese usually crowds out attempts at understanding and tolerance, and leaves mostly resentment.

Cheng himself came from Beijing, held a broader outlook, and as a painter, calligrapher, poet, doctor of Chinese medicine, and master of tai chi chuan, had considerable accomplishments to his credit. Some of the New York Chinese, as a consequence, envied and resented him. More than once Cheng clashed with some of Chinatown's leaders over one matter or another, not all of which were concerned with tai chi, reportedly with tempers on both sides flaring. At any rate, Cheng recognized tai chi's value for all races and nationalities (with the exception of the Japanese, whom he viewed with a jaundiced eye because of his experience with them in China in the thirties and forties) and was intent on spreading his tai chi throughout the world.

The Chinese in Chinatown who attended Cheng's classes were unprepared for the flood of non-Chinese who came to learn tai chi or for Cheng's popularity as a teacher. To their dismay, they soon found themselves only a small minority in the school. They asked for and were granted one day of the week on which only Chinese could come to practice.

This situation continued over a few years until Cheng decided to return to Taiwan for an indefinite stay of at least a year. He expected classes at his school to continue during his absence and we understood that he would eventually return to resume teaching. But as soon as he left, the Chinese changed the front door lock and suspended classes, to the rude surprise of the many non-Chinese who were studying there. To counter this unexpected move and to hold the predominantly non-Chinese segment of the school together, those of us who had been teaching continued the class schedule at various locations until we found a suitable loft of our own. I should add that in all of this a few Chinese remained loyal to Cheng, despite the possibility that this loyalty might prove costly to them in their business dealings in the Chinese community.

After a year and a half, Cheng returned to New York and to a school that his senior students had preserved and made to thrive at a new location. He remained here for about eighteen months and then returned to Taiwan, where in the spring of 1975 he died. Some months after his death, Cheng's organization began to come apart. Cheng had groomed seven of his senior students for the leadership of the tai chi school, in the hope that their combined strengths would equal his and allow the school to grow and to flourish. But the seven were not really of like mind about how the organization should be run, nor were they personally compatible. They had come together and held together because of their interest in Cheng's teaching. Soon after he died and they realized he was not going to return, a couple of them attempted to wrest control of the organization from the others. Feelings ran high, and there was even some legal skirmishing.

This turn of events was certainly an unpleasant and unfortunate interlude in the transmission to the West of Cheng's valuable brand of tai chi. Also, the behavior of some of Cheng's senior students seemed to me, at the time, out of step with the tenets of Taoist and Confucian philosophy, which he had been trying for some time to teach them.

If studying the martial arts for a number of years is supposed to effect salutary changes in us on the levels of mind and spirit as well as on the physical level, do our actions in everyday life reflect these changes? I did not observe the individuals involved in the three cases described above for a long enough time or closely enough to say very much about how they were changing or developing. Also, to delineate and contrast the many cultural differences between the members of these groups goes far beyond the scope of this discussion and can be found in more than sufficient detail elsewhere. By and large, however, these people seemed to act more in accord with their cultural conditioning than with their martial arts training.

How, then, did their training manifest itself? Perhaps in their acting with strength, toughness, and confidence in themselves and in the correctness of their positions. In addition to such strong-mindedness, we could expect their training to produce in them depth and breadth of understanding sufficient to allow them to accommodate a point of view at variance with their own. This was, however, far from universally the case.

One of the ideas that many martial artists hold dear is that if we can find "the way," this discovery and the understanding it brings will permeate all aspects of our life. "The way" can be found through correct and diligent training over a long period of time. Probably we cannot really discern this achievement in another without having ourselves achieved it. Nevertheless, my stage of development at the time allowed me to see little evidence of the kind of self-realization in question. But, then, perhaps the training of most of these martial artists was of a kind that stressed the development of fighting skill and competitiveness and did not lead practitioners beyond, or help them to see, the limitations of such an approach.

As for evidence of spiritual development in these people, it was nearly impossible to ascertain this from their behavior. But how do we determine the existence or the degree of someone's spiritual realization? The closest I have come to sensing such a development in someone—and I include in this category Zen masters and other "holy" men as well as accomplished martial artists—is the feeling they give off of quietness, settledness, and balanced energy. Some of the actors in the events I described may well have been, to some degree at least, spiritually developed, but their participation in these events, and their having to function in a somewhat unfamiliar and hostile environment, may have served to disturb or mask their development.

Though we may hope for more from martial arts training, we need not disparage development that will allow us to pursue our interests with strength, toughness, and perseverance. There seems nothing wrong with self-interest either, if it is broad enough in outlook to allow an individual to seek the welfare of everyone involved in a situation, understand the issues, and be able to anticipate the course of events. The self-interest of many of these people, however, appeared directed primarily toward securing immediate advantage for only their own small group. Moreover, their training, in most cases, seemed not to have enabled them to break the hold of their conditioning.

Should I have been able to determine from their actions and statements how, and to what extent, their martial arts training affected the people described in the foregoing situations? I would have to say no. Although, at the time, I expected their years of training to have produced in them a considerable degree of maturity and wisdom, I should have withheld judgment. After all, I didn't know what qualities of mind they started with and to what degree other factors in their lives influenced them. Nor did I know their training's direction, intensity, and duration. Finally, my assessment was not free of subjectivity, and what I thought I noticed in these persons may well have been distorted by my particular beliefs and expectations.

Is it possible that martial arts training has very little spiritual effect on its practitioners and that they will develop largely in accordance with their individual psychological makeup, their social interactions, and their general cultural conditioning? Though it is true that by the time we begin martial arts training we have already been formed by our nature and conditioning, it appears that training can still bring about significant positive change. I base this statement on my observation of behavioral changes in fellow martial artists and in my own students over a period of years, on the statements of these people concerning their feelings about the effect on them of their training, and most important, on the changes I have noticed in myself.

Of course, if we wished to be somewhat scientific in trying to determine the effect of our training on students, we might try to set up a study in which one of two groups would receive years of martial arts training and the other none. The behavior of the two groups in a given situation could then be compared and conclusions drawn. But we would have to ensure that all the individuals constituting the groups had a similar basic mental and physical makeup. To do all this seems a difficult but not impossible task. But it is highly improbable that such a study would be considered of sufficient importance to warrant funding.

Perhaps we could devise a psychological profile of some sort that could be administered at the outset and then at five-year intervals to a group of fledgling martial artists. Through this instrument we would try to determine what changes took place in them as they continued their training. To my knowledge, no one has done this, and it is not certain that we would really be able to measure what we want because of the many inconstant or fluctuating variables involved.

Proceeding, then, to my observations of changes over the years in martial arts practitioners and in my students, the growth of mental qualities like alertness, determination, perseverance, and self-confidence seemed to rise from an increase in their strength, agility, and coordination, and from their development of skill. In some this general strengthening manifested itself mainly in increased assertiveness and sometimes stubbornness with regard to maintaining a point of view or an intellectual position. In others, it appeared gradually in the form of a more settled and quiet demeanor. In addition, some became more stoical and showed little regard for the welfare of their body, thinking that they must not allow themselves to give in to such minor annoyances as pulled muscles or torn ligaments. Others moved toward greater awareness of their body's messages and modified their behavior in accord with such information. In individuals there were, of course, combinations of these attributes as well as the demonstration of one or another attribute on different occasions. It is quite possible, also, that these men already possessed these qualities and attributes and that their training functioned to bring them out.

The statements of my students over the years support the foregoing observations about the largely salutary surface changes I have noticed in them. In addition, they have supplied information on less easily discernible positive developments in the way they relate to others and live their lives. Many think their training has allowed them to practice ways of letting go of fixed ideas and of trying to achieve their ends by harmonizing with the forces around them, as well as other useful and desirable ways of relating to the world. They would probably have encountered such ideas as time went by, but a large gap exists between an intellectual apprehension of a concept and a physical and emotional experience of it, let alone its internalization.

As for changes in myself, the effects of training I have observed in other martial artists and heard about from them are part of my experience too. In addition, to a greater or lesser degree, I believe I have been influenced by all the possibilities for development on various levels that I mention in this book.

For each of us what is ultimately of most importance, both in our actual training and in our attempt to assess the value of this training, is to focus on ourselves. This is not meant in the sense of a selfish preoccupation or a lessening of our ability to sense what others are doing or feeling and what is going on around us. Rather, it means that we should not compare ourselves with others in terms of innate ability or quality or in the progress we or they are making. Instead, we should determinedly and single-mindedly work on ourselves in line with the principles of our discipline or art. Also, it means that attempts to assess the extent of another's development, or the worth of another system of training, are far inferior to an honest awareness and appraisal of the effect of our training on ourselves. If we have given our training a full measure of our efforts over a few years and are displeased with our level of achievement or with other aspects of the art, it may be well to conclude it, to go elsewhere, or to proceed on our own. But if we believe we are making satisfactory progress, that there is more to learn, and above all, that we are enjoying the process, we should continue our practice.

CHAPTER IX

Health, Diet, and Drugs

> This truth is to be lived, it is not to be merely pronounced with the mouth.....
>
> There is really nothing to argue about in this teaching; Any arguing is sure to go against the intent of it.
>
> Doctrines given up to controversy and argumentation lead of themselves to birth and death.
>
> HUI NENG

MANY OF THOSE who engage in martial arts training do so for reasons of health. They are aware of studies that prove exercising makes people feel better and live longer. Given their interest in this area, they will also have noticed suggestions for a healthy diet and might have sought out special foods or ways of eating aimed at enhancing athletic performance. Perhaps, also, they have heard that eating certain foods or even taking drugs might give them spiritual insight.

In the earlier decades of the twentieth century, statements about the salutary influence of proper diet and exercise on health were thought to be the mistaken conceptions of people outside orthodox medicine. Consequently, such ideas were generally dismissed as fads, as were recommendations of dietary practices that might contribute to spiritual awakening.

My early thoughts about health and food ran toward the romantic idea that what is natural, primitive, in its wild state, or unadulterated is preferable to or purer than what has gone through some sort of processing. This notion may not really survive critical examination, but it may help to explain my search for natural ways of preventing illness and of curing it when it occurred. Moreover, even when I got sick, which happened rarely, I was reluctant to consult doctors or to take the drugs they prescribed.

This inclination and attitude received major support when I encountered, a couple of decades ago, attacks on the germ theory of illness. The germ theory holds that we become ill because we are attacked by bacteria, which must be destroyed in order to restore us to health. An explanation of illness that I found much more plausible is that it results mainly from a poor diet and/or a poor environment. Over time these conditions create toxins that overwhelm those internal organs whose function it is to eliminate them. The outcome is a breakdown in the system. The drugs usually prescribed to help us get well may give an apparently quick cure, but usually only the symptoms are relieved and the underlying causes remain. In addition, the side effects of the drugs may give us other health problems. If the main causes of our illness are not treated by changing the way we eat and live, our lives can be not only miserable but considerably shortened as well.

This, to me, more plausible theory about illness and its prevention and cure has in the last few years received indirect support from other sources. For example, writers on the value of exercise in maintaining good health have also included dietary suggestions in their proposed regimens. Even the mainstream medical fraternity has become more aware of the connection between the food we eat and illness. Doctors have begun to recommend, in much larger numbers than a generation or two ago, dietary practices that will help us to get better if we are already ill and to prevent illness if we are well. Twenty or thirty years ago food and diet were treated by physicians and most experts on health as of minor importance as long as one got what was considered a "balanced" diet. This balance, of course, reflected a Western cultural bias by including much larger quantities of animal protein than are consumed elsewhere in the world. Finally, the dietary criticism of refined food products is today no longer solely the domain of food faddists.

In my twenties and thirties, when I was concerned with building and maintaining physical strength and energy for playing judo and karate, and for earning a living, I must say that I paid only minor attention to what I was eating as long as I liked the taste and there was enough of it. I left the decisions as to what we got to eat to my wife, who had become interested in nutrition and followed the advice of Adelle Davis, an advocate of a high-protein diet. As a result, we often ate a large breakfast, usually including meat (beef liver was especially favored), and I drank supplemental protein drinks the main ingredient of which was brewer's yeast. We ate sugars and starches in at least average quantities but also consumed more than our share of fruits and vegetables. During the couple of decades over which we adhered to this diet I felt generally healthy, strong, and energetic.

But my good health may have been more a product of a basically strong constitution and lots of physical activity rather than our diet, because toward the end of this period of time my wife began to suffer from hemorrhoids, severe headaches lasting a full day, and then asthma. While looking for ways to alleviate these conditions, she discovered the books of medical doctors and nutritionists (Norman W. Walker, Max Gerson, and Max Bircher-Benner, among others) who used diet to cure various illnesses. These writers theorized that substances foreign to the body, like additives in processed foods and chemicals and pollutants in the environment, are toxic and, if our body cannot eliminate them, undermine our health. They held that cooking food reduced or eliminated essential nutrients. In general, they favored a vegetarian diet and raw foods and through these means cured thousands who had sought help from traditional allopathic medicine to no avail.

My wife began to treat herself by changing and controlling her diet and gradually cured herself of hemorrhoids and headaches. Further, she found that maintaining a rather strict vegetarian diet reduced or eliminated her breathing problems. But she encountered difficulty in remaining faithful to her regimen for more than short periods.

Her results and her urging influenced me to try to move in the direction she had gone. I wanted to maintain the good health I had enjoyed until then and felt a little concern that my wife's health problems or others might soon become mine. I found that her diet, when I followed it—and I did not follow it with anywhere near the strictness its adherents prescribed—seemed to provide additional lightness of body and clarity of mind. Because I had seldom been ill and felt no physical limitations on what I wanted to do, I still did not watch what I ate too closely. As I got older, however,

I must say that overeating or eating combinations of foods that digested poorly together, or at different rates of speed, sometimes caused me considerable discomfort. Naturally, on those occasions, I resolved to eat more carefully in the future.

My wife also began to experiment with drinking vegetable juices. The naturopath Norman W. Walker (mentioned above) had made a strong case for a diet of raw food, in correct combinations, and lots of vegetable juices as conducive to good health and longevity. He did not limit his advice to food but also suggested exercise, colonic irrigation, and other health measures. His recommendations carried considerable weight, because he had cured himself of illness through his diet and lived to be 109 years old. My understanding is that toward his last years he was still working and in reasonably full possession of his mental and physical faculties.

My interest in esoteric disciplines brought me into contact with dietary prescriptions for promoting better health and providing optimum conditions for their adherents' spiritual development. The food we ate in the Soto Zen monastery in Japan where I sat for some months was thought to play its part in our efforts. For a while I taught tai chi to a macrobiotic food group in Boston whose members practiced their diet in the belief that improvements in their health would be mental as well as physical and would gradually lead to a better world order. My experience with yoga training over the last couple of years also made me more aware that a vegetarian diet and what are termed *sattvic* foods contribute to the health and purification of the body and help to promote spiritual growth. Even the organized religions address issues of health and spirituality by proscribing the eating of some animals and of certain other foods or by instituting fasting on particular days of the week or over a few periods during the year.

The cultural differences in food consumption and in ideas of what constitutes a good diet are somewhat disturbing to those who seek a universally recognized diet that will allow them to function optimally. In many cases, dietary philosophies contradict one another completely. In the West, we believe that to enjoy good health we need a balanced diet with a relatively large amount of animal protein and a variety of foods that will provide us a whole range of vitamins and minerals. Yet people in some other parts of the world eat very little of a limited number of foods and manage not only to survive but to live long and productive lives. I have even heard of a woman who, without apparent ill effect, has subsisted for years on little more than one sacramental wafer each day. Indian yogis are reputed to lead their lives ingesting nothing but a few pieces of fruit and a glass of buffalo milk daily. In our society, we are told to chew our food many times before swallowing, because this practice aids digestion. Yet, G. I. Gurdjieff, in his travels, met a teacher who advocated little chewing of food because he believed that the internal system required exercise and would be strengthened if it were given work to do and weakened to the point of breakdown if denied such exercise. The value of fasting—giving the digestive system a rest and thereby releasing energy for spiritual growth and for self-healing—seems to be universally recognized, but opinions differ on the optimum length of the fast.

Cheng, my tai chi teacher, favored soft-cooked rice, accompanied by various cooked vegetables, meat, or fish and ate little or nothing after three P.M. I have heard of monks who were permitted to eat all they wished until noon and then not again until they woke the following morning. This regimen was said to keep them thin and in good health.

It is, then, apparent that many contradictory pronouncements have been made about diet and nutrition. To explain these contradictions, some people have theorized that it is our beliefs about the food we eat that are of greatest importance. Thus, if we believe we need large quantities of certain foods to be healthy, the lack of these foods could make us ill. On the other hand, we might enjoy good health if we believe our diet is adequate even if it seems below par by some standards. There seems little doubt that our eating habits have a mental as well as a physical basis.

How much attention should we pay to this subject of nutrition? Among my acquaintances have been a number of people who were almost obsessed with food intake, and sometimes with its elimination. In general, the health of these people was not good, nor did it improve significantly over the years as a result of their preoccupation. This is a subjective judgment and may be too extreme, but they did seem to overemphasize diet in their lives and did not appear to benefit by this practice.

As we take all the above observations into account, what conclusions seem warranted? It would seem that the choice of which foods to eat, at which times, and in which combinations is a matter best left to individual need and inclination. We must learn to notice the effect on our body and mind of what we eat and drink and then make whatever changes are necessary until we reach a diet that allows us to feel and function well. Our diet should, as with all the concerns of our lives, receive an appropriate but not disproportionate share of our attention.

Unfortunately, becoming observant about our eating habits and their effect does not completely solve our problems in this area, because the results of eating certain foods may not be felt for many years. Also, even if we notice that some foods seem to do us little good, we may like them and find ourselves unable to let them alone. Thus, without self-discipline the value of observation is much reduced. The situation is even more complicated when we hear of or see people who appear to be breaking dietary recommendations with impunity. I know personally of people who ate poorly in terms of the average nutritionist's prescriptions but who lived into their eighties. They neither fasted nor were they vegetarians.

In my own case, as I became more aware of my mind and body processes I saw clearly that my physical condition affected my mental and emotional functioning to a considerable degree. People are capable of transcending physical ailments, but my experience has been that poor physical condition makes everything else we do more difficult. That is, we seem to set ourselves an added handicap in whatever we are doing, mentally or physically, by giving insufficient attention to our physical health.

More specifically, I seem to feel better when I avoid eating red meat or, for that matter, any kind of meat. Seeds, nuts, and soybean curd have proved excellent substitutes for meat protein. I believe vegetables and fruits are beneficial, and I eat these daily in rather large quantities. Over the last few years I have drunk a quart of vegetable (mostly a combination of carrot and spinach, or carrot and celery) juice daily, with increasingly good results.

I am partial to the theory that my beliefs about food play an important role in the food's effect on me. But I have no real or complete knowledge of how my body processes what I eat nor of the interplay of mind and body in this processing. I can only base my tentative conclusions about food on how what I eat seems to affect me.

I might add that although the kind and quantity of food we eat, how we combine our food, the timing of meals, and our beliefs about food can, over time, affect our health and well-being, these factors are not the primary ones responsible for our development on various levels in martial arts. Nutrition, important though it is, is no substitute for hard and steady training. It is probably misguided to attempt to discover a diet or foods that will act magically to provide us with endurance, strength, or understanding. Yet many competitive martial artists will probably be unable to resist looking to better nutrition or to some magic food or vitamin as a way to gain a slight advantage over their opponents.

Attempts to enhance performance may even move some beyond the bounds of nutritional considerations to experimentation with various drugs. Steroids, for example, seem to give their users something extra, enabling them to surpass their previous best efforts and, of course, the efforts of many other competitors. Unfortunately, steroid use is illegal and probably dangerous to an athlete's health. It also reflects the outlook of those athletes who believe that victory is of first importance and worth almost any price. Hopefully those in the sportive martial arts will recognize that winning is secondary to their growth in other areas, making the use of performance-enhancing drugs valueless or unattractive.

As for achieving enlightenment, the observance of dietary laws of one kind or another in itself does not appear to ensure it. Nevertheless, for those who believe that the purification of the body is of value, or a prerequisite, in heightening perception, paying attention to and controlling one's food intake becomes of some importance. Also, it is probably reasonable to think that improperly nourishing or caring for the body can impede mental or spiritual development.

Fasting has, in some cultures, been thought a necessity for visionary quests. Those drawn toward the role of shaman in primitive society underwent a long fast as well as other austerities. My experience with involuntary fasting occurred in the 1940s when I was aboard a submarine that was forced to run on the surface during a severe week-long storm. I suffered from seasickness and could eat nothing. My dreams and fantasies centered on food and were extremely clear and vivid. This clarity and vividness might have run to less mundane subjects had I sought or expected to see a spiritual manifestation of some sort. It is also quite possible that what we see under these conditions comes under the heading of hallucination rather than revelation or insight. Therefore, I believe that except for fasts of a few days at most, which can have a therapeutic physical and mental effect, moderation in the area of nutrition ultimately will allow us to come to whatever realizations lie within our capabilities. Nevertheless, as concerns moderation in food consumption, clarity of vision for persons in our society seems to be enhanced, in general, by eating less rather than more.

Those interested in the growth of awareness have often been attracted to the ingestion of psychedelic drugs for the purpose of consciousness alteration or expansion. I have never liked the idea of using them, perhaps because of the disinclination, expressed earlier, to take drugs even to cure illness. Also, my martial arts training was from the outset aimed toward strengthening my body and mind, and drugs seem to me to go in another direction altogether.

Many who favor psychedelic drugs feel that their use could help us break out of our accustomed mode of viewing the world. The more moderate among the drug advocates hold that taking them might not permanently alter our thinking, but it might bring about the insight that the world is not ordered at all and that each culture attempts to establish its own arbitrary stamp on what is out there. Still other drug takers admit that even if drugs can help us alter our view of reality, we are afforded only a momentary glimpse of other possibilities. To bring a real and lasting change into one's life seems to require a long-term training approach. I was firmly enough established in attempts to expand consciousness through meditation to reject the use of drugs for this purpose. Also, I feared that taking large drug doses might disturb the mind's functioning on the important everyday level.

My reservations about drugs also supported, or were supported by, a theory I subscribed to concerning the functioning of the conscious mind. The theory maintained that our conscious mind is capable of handling both an analytical, rational approach to the world and an intuitive, holistic one, and, in fact, synthesizes these all the time if we allow it to do so. I thought increasing one's clarity of mind and vision along the lines suggested by this theory a worthwhile pursuit, and felt that drugs detracted from this goal.

86

A fairer attitude might have been to try these drugs for myself before I came to any conclusions about their usefulness. A factor that added to my reluctance to do this was that the people I met or knew who had used psychedelic drugs did not, in general, seem to be in a mental or physical state I found transcendent or appealing.

Distinctions have been made between drugs made from chemicals and drugs derived from plants. American Indians, in religious ceremonies that are attempts at illumination, use moderate amounts of such plants as peyote. It is said that such natural hallucinogens do not affect the human system adversely to the extent chemicals do. Such a practice seemed not unattractive, at least at first hearing. But bound up as it appeared to be with a different cultural approach to life from mine, it would have raised all those issues that come with an attempt to pull one element out of an integrated whole. By itself this element loses the support of the rest of the culture and usually becomes something other than it was.

I suppose I had nothing to do with drugs because intuitively I didn't feel right about using them. I have heard apparently logical appearing arguments in their favor, and if I endorsed the use of drugs as a different way of experiencing the world, I would, no doubt, quote such arguments. But I did not and do not endorse them. In addition, other than such an occurrence as a spontaneous full illumination, flashes of insight seem to come periodically and seem to be encouraged or promoted by training over the years. Even where it appears that full enlightenment has come suddenly, closer examination usually reveals that the ground has been prepared over time. Moreover, if the new vision of the world is not to grow dim, it must be nourished by some kind of continuing work. Using drugs as an alternative to training, or even as an aid to speed up change, doesn't seem to give nearly the same result.

CHAPTER X

The Ideal *Dojo*

> A man is supple and weak when living, but hard
> and stiff when dead. Grass and trees are pliant
> and fragile when living, but dried and shriveled
> when dead. Thus the hard and strong are the
> comrades of death; the supple and the weak are
> the comrades of life.
>
> LAO TZU

THE FOREGOING CHAPTERS suggest ways of proceeding optimally for those who wish to develop themselves spiritually and mentally as well as physically through martial arts. In this chapter I would like to discuss the mix of students at the martial arts *dojo*. This mix can contribute to or detract from an atmosphere conducive to the kind of development in question. The conception of the general public about schools of martial arts is that one goes there in order to learn to defend oneself. Movies and television often dramatize and elaborate on the process by showing the "good" guy, who had earlier been bullied, fighting with and overcoming the "bad" guy after a few months of practice. The fledgling martial artist is sometimes shown competing in a tournament and perhaps gaining promotion to a higher grade. The emphasis is on physicality, with such character qualities as determination and courage playing a helping part. Sometimes moviemakers also touch briefly and shallowly on exotic philosophical and cultural patterns of relating to the world.

But training need not emphasize preparation for fighting or competition and the heavy physical workout and punishment that usually accompany them. Hard sportive training tends to attract younger people whose bodies can stand the strain and who seek out challenge and situations in which they can prove, or learn about, themselves. Unfortunately, a *dojo* where such players predominate is seldom attractive to players who are not young and strong. Nor does it seem appropriate for children or for women, except for the unusually athletic or fit. Of greatest benefit to society and to the individuals who constitute it would be a *dojo* where everyone could train, the young and the old of both sexes. This seems to have been Jigoro Kano's plan when he first formulated his ideas about judo.

When a martial art serves primarily as a sport, the general pattern characteristic of sports in our society holds sway—a relatively few compete and the great majority act as spectators. But the benefits martial arts practice confers come through participation and not through the vicarious thrill and excitement of identification with competitors. People of all ages should be able to practice one of the martial arts and appreciate at first hand the various changes in themselves such training can bring about. How would such a *dojo* operate?

Obviously, competition and preparation for it would be deemphasized. Students who wished to compete could do so periodically, and almost everyone should be able to experience competition at some time. But perhaps two outside tournaments a year would be sufficient to enable players to feel the added stress of this activity and to assess their functioning under these conditions. To prepare for such tournaments, some practice matches could be held in the *dojo*. Children should probably not be encouraged to compete until they are well into their teens; even though contests for quite young children in some martial arts have been promoted.

It may be appropriate at this point to discuss children's martial arts training in greater detail. I don't believe it is in their best interest to have them practice in classes designed exclusively for children. I taught children's judo classes for a time in the late fifties. Classes were made up of boys aged seven up to about fifteen. In a class of ten or twelve boys, only two or three were of approximately the same age and size, giving little support to the idea that in a children's class the students would be somewhat homogeneous and therefore better able to practice together. Some boys were there because their parents had sent them, in the belief that they needed toughening up or lessons in self-defense. These boys were generally the youngest and least athletic in the class, lacked interest in judo, and often had trouble paying attention. Sometimes the parents of these younger boys watched the class and by their presence undermined the teacher-student relationship.

If children are, however, enrolled in adult classes, they should not begin formal training until they are thirteen or fourteen. At an earlier age their rather short attention span and their somewhat fragile body development could well contribute to injury. When their bodies become stronger, they are better able to stand the strain of the repetitive, fully focused punches and kicks of boxing or a twisting, turning throw in judo. A softer martial art like aikido or tai chi chuan would probably not be harmful to children, but relatively few find sufficient appeal or attraction in these softer arts.

If children younger than thirteen show a strong interest in learning a martial art, or if their parents wish to have them undergo such training, the children should be shown and encouraged to do basic exercises designed for all-around physical development. They should be taught and allowed to practice only those martial arts techniques that are unlikely to injure their still-developing bodies. Practicing with adults more frequently than with other children should help them to avoid injury and also instill respect for the art they are learning. Some of the rituals—like bowing as one enters and leaves the *dojo*, behaving with decorum and restraint, and bowing to the teacher and to other students—can help children develop a sense of the importance of things other than themselves. When children do practice together, they should do so under the watchful eye of the teacher or of an adult senior student.

If parents are not themselves involved in martial arts and cannot supervise their children's practice, it is important for them to choose the right *dojo* for their children, because there may be considerable variation in the philosophy of martial arts teachers. Parents should become aware of the teacher's thoughts regarding such issues as an individual's concern for the welfare of others and the circumstances in which violence might be justified. That is, if the teacher encourages his students to apply their techniques strongly with little consideration for their training partners or does not prohibit their fighting on the street, parents might well avoid such a *dojo*.

When children train with adults, they may be in a better position to sense and to absorb the mental qualities martial arts training can instill.

Among these is an alertness, an ability to sense an impending confrontation early enough to avoid it or prepare adequate countermeasures. They will realize that fighting is not just a matter of physical strength and skill but includes mental toughness, the ability to assess a situation quickly and correctly, and proper planning and tactics. Moreover, the training should not put them into a state of mind where their response to an impending attack, especially against a superior force of multiple or armed opponents, is to stand and fight rather than retreat. Sometimes circumstances seem to demand instant action, which might later be considered heroic or assigned other labels, such as "brave" or "valiant." But where there is time to consider alternatives, preserving oneself should rank high in importance and taking unnecessary risks or disregarding danger should be thought foolish rather than anything else. For example, police are trained, at least in the more enlightened forces, to avoid taking individual action in subduing or taking into custody individuals or groups who are well armed or numerically superior. Tracking the movements of these persons, or containing them, until reinforcements arrive ususally gets the job done with far fewer injuries and deaths of both police and criminals.

This approach may mean that children must sometimes restrict their movements to avoid confrontation or, meeting with danger from others, must back away from it if they see only slim chances of emerging intact. But they should consider such maneuvering as part of mental training, a chance to develop qualities of mind that can help them outwit those who may wish to harm them. If their teacher and the advanced adult students understand the potential for self-development in many of the volatile situations teenagers encounter, children can make a great deal of progress on important nonphysical levels. Being in touch with mature, balanced, and trained minds can be advantageous for children's development, especially for those whose parents are narrow or shallow in outlook, or children whose ideas about life come primarily from their peers.

Returning again to the issue of competition, the foregoing remarks on the harmful effect of competition on adults apply with equal force, or perhaps even more force, to children. Though it is also a matter of individual temperament and outlook, the pressure felt by competitors in martial arts tournaments is probably greater than that felt by participants in team sports.

In the latter, the blame for losing is more widely spread, and team members can provide one another comfort and emotional support. Even in a close game when a crucial error made by one member of the team might be blamed for the loss, that player is never as alone as the martial artist in one-to-one competition. If the martial artist loses he usually blames himself, if he has that sort of outlook or turn of mind. Also his parents, depending on the extent to which they may identify with him or are living through him, may consider a poor performance cause for withholding affection. Such behavior on the part of the parents obviously creates a great deal of pressure or stress on a child. Nor does winning always relieve this pressure, because in the background lurks the specter of possible defeat in coming matches.

As to the particular magic that some have said infuses the world of children, by the time they are in their early teens this has usually departed. Probably this quality is only present in children before they enter school. Whether their world view in this early period of their lives squares with reality is open to question, but it is likely that when children are in their teens they will be trying to arrange their thinking and their lives to accord with the generally accepted adult patterns in their culture. Unfortunately, these patterns lean in our culture far too strongly toward ignoring or negating any aspect of life that our limited senses and intellect cannot apprehend. Moreover, we often try to reduce whatever we can grasp to mechanical principles. The magical nature of reality is then usually lost. Martial arts practice pursued meditatively can help our minds open to the magical and miraculous in life. But this opening is on a more mature level than it is in young children. Teenagers can well use this kind of training to help balance the limiting nature of the acculturation they must undergo.

My own children, a boy and a girl, grew up in a kind of martial arts environment. They were a year apart in age. Before they were five, I took them to watch classes I taught or attended. For years we went to Japanese samurai movies in which martial arts action and warrior codes and values were featured. Often we would go to a nearby park, where I did supplementary exercises for judo and karate; they would hang from my legs when I did chinups or sit on my back in pushups. At two or three years of age they also began to do these exercises. As they grew older they participated in my classes, my son doing judo and karate and my daughter karate. When we were in Japan and they were about ten, they spent about a year practicing kendo at a local *dojo*. They began martial arts before the age I recommend, but I watched their progress to be sure they didn't hurt themselves. On the other hand, I wanted them to experience the physical and mental discipline of martial arts, because I thought their general education lacked these elements.

Neither child was always enthusiastic about attending my classes on a regular basis. After all, I was the teacher and I probably expected more of them that I should have. They did not, however, actively resist attending class. Nevertheless, my son moved into other sports in high school, although he again practiced judo for a while in his early thirties. My daughter learned tai chi, practiced push-hands with me over the years, and even instructed some classes in the tai chi form.

The physical strengthening they underwent, the skills they learned, and the point of view they absorbed through their martial arts practice all seem to have benefited them. It might have been better for me to have sent them to another teacher instead of having them attend my classes. This is generally the tradition in Japan when a father runs a martial arts *dojo*. But we moved to different locations in different parts of the world while they were growing up and it seemed more convenient to have them come to my classes.

What about martial arts training for people at the other end of the age spectrum? Of the four arts I have personally experienced, tai chi chuan and aikido seem to lend themselves reasonably well to continued practice into our sixth and seventh decades.

Judo, as originally conceived, was for the old as well as the young, but when it became a sport the hard training for competition made it suitable mostly for young players. Older physiques, especially the knee joints, are best not subjected to the stress of standing techniques. *Makikomi* judo throws where both players crash to the mat, sometimes one landing on the other, are not conducive to the health of an aging body. Nevertheless, seniors who have developed skill in judo mat work can be more than a match for their younger opponents. I remember practicing mat work at the Kodokan in Japan with men in their fifties and sixties who, seemingly without effort, were able to establish and maintain control of me.

Can we do karate as we get older? I found that I could continue quite strenuous noncontact sparring through my fifties. But full-contact karate is best left to much younger players whose bodies are resilient enough to withstand, at least for a time, that kind of abuse.

Theoretically, if we intend to use martial arts as a method of working on, or of liberating, ourselves, we may think it unimportant whether or not we choose an art that is physically taxing. We may even believe that the rigor and intensity of hard training will speed our progress to our goal. But practically speaking, the injuries we suffer are an unnecessary additional burden, all the more so if we are older and the injuries take a long time to heal. Making an already difficult task even harder seems of questionable value.

People who have spent some decades in martial arts are in a good position to assess the effect on themselves of the methods they have used to further their progress. Some might notice that the results they desired from their training at the outset were shallow and limited, and achieving them sometimes physically and mentally harmful. If they continued to practice the same martial art, their accumulation of skill and experience, a decline in their physical capabilities, and a quieting of youthful drives may well have caused them to recognize the value of a different approach to training. To make such a change, some may have switched to another martial art—one that helped them to concentrate on refinements of technique or mental development.

In addition, their training will have affected their beliefs about themselves and about life, so that when they contrast the beliefs they held during their first years with those they hold today they may notice rather wide variations. Some of these variations can be attributed to their being different people today than they were thirty or forty years ago. Youthful energy and drive diminish as we grow older. Hormonal changes in us, no doubt, bear some degree of responsibility for an altered outlook. Nevertheless, everyone over fifty or sixty years of age does not think alike or hold the same beliefs. Those who have undergone a few decades of martial arts training with qualified teachers have a good chance of reaching those timeless understandings about life that go far beyond the shallow clichés in vogue at any given time.

As I review my judo and karate training, I feel, in general, pleased with the effect it has had on me. From my present perspective, however, I think I would have been better off had I approached my training in a way that deemphasized strength and concentrated on technique. Put another way, I might have profited by applying the tai chi principles I came to later in life to both of the harder disciplines. Yet, I don't know whether or not I could or would have spent the required years in training that would have been necessary to bring me to a level of accomplishment satisfying to me. When I began practicing, I wanted as quickly as possible to be recognized as a tough opponent. Because I was already stronger than average, I chose the route of power as the fastest way to my goal. I did not neglect technique, but where I had the option of choosing between spending additional time practicing to refine my technique, beyond the practical and utilitarian, and doing exercises to become stronger, I chose the latter. My decision enabled me to defeat opponents whose technique may have been superior to mine and brought me success in tournaments. Of course, few of the opponents I met in my early years of judo were highly developed technicians, nor was I below the average in my technical ability.

My wish for recognition probably stemmed from my particular makeup or filled a psychological need and accorded with the attitude of most people I knew toward sports competition. I did not enjoy having to compete, but doing well in tournaments boosted my ego and, for a while at least, made me feel good. I much preferred winning to losing because it brought the rewards I sought in terms of higher rank and the admiration (at least in my estimation) of others.

This way of thinking is probably usual and "normal" in our culture, but I have come to believe that it is not a healthy one and is accompanied by a good deal of suffering. Seniors who have come to such a conclusion about martial arts training might well try to guide juniors away from a potentially harmful approach to training. If they are teachers, their influence will be even stronger. If they discourage competition and emphasize the perfection of technique and perhaps eventually of the student, their followers will have little choice but to go along.

Although my judo teacher, Yamamoto, was excellent in almost all respects, he did seem to want us to win when we entered a tournament.

Moreover, we students interpreted the *dojo* atmosphere as a competitive one in which we constantly, within set limits, tried to outdo one another. Yamamoto's attitude toward competition arose from his Japanese traditions and was not the same as ours, but even though he probably held certain Buddhist views that transcended everyday considerations of winning and losing, he did not, at that time, expound them. What he thought about competition appeared to us similar enough to our American culture's attitude toward the desirability of victory and its fruits as to make little difference. Had he stressed another training approach, especially one that seemed noncompetitive, it is difficult to say whether the students he taught would have remained with him. He might have drawn a completely different group of students. It is also possible that had Yamamoto taught his judo differently, students who originally came with the expectation of learning to fight and to compete with and overcome others might well have remained and been influenced to see themselves and the world in a different way.

It is interesting, in connection with the progression of a martial artist's development, that in his mid-forties Yamamoto became interested in aikido. Tohei, Uyeshiba's leading aikido student at the time, had come to Hawaii in the early 1950s to introduce aikido to the Islands. Yamamoto had become somewhat disappointed with the practical aspects of judo, because although he had been practicing for many years, some of his physically strong students, with just a few years of experience, were sometimes able to frustrate his techniques. He felt that his experience, developed over more than a quarter century of training, should have continued to enable him to deal easily with his students. He thought he saw in aikido a system whereby his techniques and ability could continue to grow rather than remain static or diminish over time. Also, Yamamoto was strongly attracted by the aikido philosophy. He went on to become one of the leading Hawaii aikido teachers, instructing students into his seventies.

To summarize, martial artists in their fifth or sixth decades are obviously in a good position to view the effect of their years of practice on their body, mind, and spirit. In looking back, they will be able to see which training was of greatest benefit to them, which had only minor effect, and which was detrimental. In the *dojo*, they can pass on their wisdom to juniors. Unfortunately, we must be ready if we are really to grasp or understand the import of even the wisest of councils. If we are unprepared for or not receptive to an idea, merely hearing it will make little immediate difference. Juniors may want or need actually to experience an overly strong dose of competition with all its negative aspects, as well as other undesirable results of misdirected training that seniors may have learned are best shunned. Nevertheless, it is valuable for juniors to come into contact with the seniors' point of view. As time passes, changes in the juniors' circumstances may allow them to open to and to begin to understand the seniors' words.

I believe women should practice with men and not only with other women. When men and women practice together, each can come to know the other's strengths and weaknesses and can work on developing techniques or methods most suited to dealing with them. As technique improves physical attributes and gender become less important and it becomes a matter of assessing or sensing each individual opponent's capabilities and applying an appropriate response.

As stated earlier, in the give-and-take of practice individuals are afforded a good chance to get to know one another, stripped of the layer of language and accepted social behavior that we often use to disguise our true nature, especially in our relations with the opposite sex. Although martial arts practice is not free of rules and behavior patterns, players are attempting to do their best against one another. Thus, their interests are opposed, and under this kind of stress an individual's true character is much more easily discernible.

During my years of training in martial arts I met with few examples of the kind of *dojo* I have tried to describe. Most *dojo* seemed strongly competition-oriented—a direction that usually excluded or gave only minimal attention to those who were not young and strong. But where tournament participation was not stressed or was absent, instruction was usually mediocre or of a very slack nature.

Nevertheless, an approximation of the ideal I suggest is possible. The closest approaches to it I have personally encountered were in New York City—in Cheng Man-ching's tai chi group and in George Yoshida's judo club. I was introduced to Cheng's tai chi at an open house held on the day of a Chinese political celebration observed each year on October 10.

Some of the students displayed their techniques and we shared the food and drink provided by the group. Students there were both male and female and ranged in age from teenagers to people in their sixties. The relaxed atmosphere that prevailed both surprised and impressed me. I had been accustomed to a much more formal and somewhat stiff Japanese way of presenting a martial arts demonstration. To my mind, this Chinese martial arts system and its practitioners certainly seemed to demonstrate a Taoist way of doing things in an easygoing and low-keyed way.

As for George Yoshida's judo club, when he started it at Sokol Hall in New York City there was almost no judo in the area. He offered the kind of judo suitable for people who had to go to work and to make a living the morning after a practice session and could not, therefore, afford to be hurt. He discouraged the judo we have come to be familiar with— a hard, competitive orientation suitable for the young and strong who, perhaps, had not yet assumed the family or other responsibilities of the more mature. The *dojo* was located in the basement of a bar, and after practice Yoshida and many of his students would drink a few beers and discuss judo and life.

I heard of Yoshida's *dojo* when I visited New York in 1952 and met Ken Freeman, who sometimes practiced there. Freeman had gotten his training in London and was a strong player, especially in mat work. At the time, I formed no particular idea of the kind of *dojo* Yoshida ran because Freeman, who taught his own classes elsewhere, did not say too much about it. A few years later, when I was practicing judo in the San Francisco bay area, Yoshida's *dojo* was described to me by a judo player who had visited it as more of a social club than a serious place to train. His description and another negative comment I had heard in Chicago prejudiced me somewhat against Yoshida's *dojo*. But I was also strongly influenced in my unfavorable opinion by my years of judo competition and my interest in hard and serious training. Unfortunately, my way of thinking at the time was, and still is, characteristic of tournament-oriented players who wish to rise in rank. One could rise quickly by winning matches in both regular and promotional tournaments. Moreover, in the general view, success in tournaments is equated with expertise and, often, with realizing the mental and spiritual values of the training. I no longer believe that a strong player will necessarily also have developed the less visible and probably more important qualities of mind and spirit that many seek.

Thus, my feelings about Yoshida's method and its general results have over time gone from negative to fairly positive. To accommodate ambitious young players, I believe provision can be made in a *dojo* to allow them sufficient expression of youthful energy and drive. A philosophy of avoiding extremes, of living a balanced life will help channel and direct this energy and aggressiveness away from competitiveness and into areas of greater benefit both to the individual and to society. Moreover, it would be hoped that these younger players would not be the focus or get the major share of attention at a *dojo*, but rather that the needs of a much broader range of the population could be met.

CHAPTER XI

My Approach to Martial Arts Training

> When is a man in mere understanding? I answer, "When a man sees one thing separated from another." And when is a man above mere understanding? That I can tell you: "When a man sees All in all, then a man stands beyond mere understanding."
>
> ECKHART

ALTHOUGH I WAS a teacher of both judo and karate for a few decades, my main emphasis in the last twenty years has been on tai chi chuan. Through tai chi training, I believe students can derive perhaps 90 percent of the benefits martial arts can confer, with far fewer injuries. I teach Cheng Man-ching's tai chi form and a rather tame, by fighting standards, push-hands in which foot positions are fixed and opponents use the very minimum of strength to off-balance or uproot one another. Unfortunately, for students who might think that push-hands alone will confer self-defense ability, I know that someone who has no wider experience of sparring or fighting will have a difficult time of it in a real fight. Therefore, despite my reservations about students learning self-defense as a primary objective, expressed in Chapter III, I introduced this kind of training, thinking that students should have the ability and the option to be able to defend themselves from attack. Nor was this the only or even the most important reason for the inclusion of self-defense.

Our self-defense class includes techniques derived from karate, aikido, and judo. The class is limited to those who have completed at least a year of push-hands and it concentrates on karate. Strong karate punches and kicks are, however, neutralized by allowing them to slip past or by smothering them with soft blocks. We avoid blocks in which we smash a forearm into an opponent's wrist or ankle. Students work up to a sort of free sparring done at half or three-quarter speed.

Because they must learn to move their feet (generally not done in our style of push-hands) and to generate a strong attack when they assume the attacker's role, tai chi students can gain an appreciation of the power and focus other martial arts can produce. In the role of defender, they learn that they can successfully handle a strong and fast attack with methods that have tai chi training as a foundation.

At this point, it may be useful to discuss the concept of *chi* and the optimum and correct use of strength. Tai chi theory has it that we must generate in all our movements an internal or intrinsic energy, which we can utilize to hurt or heal. We develop this power by learning to relax, using only the parts of the body necessary to a movement and keeping the rest free of tension, and imagining, especially at the outset, that we feel this flow of energy in whatever we do. There is no doubt in my mind that such energy exists in all of us. Unfortunately, in tai chi we speak of *chi* in almost mystical terms, leading to a certain vagueness or confusion as students wonder what it is they feel or should feel. Certainly, focusing on *chi* while we are pushing hands or sparring inhibits action and reaction, with negative consequences.

I doubt that the conscious use of *chi* in martial arts techniques is any more efficacious than the power generated without such focus. Anything we do must involve the body's kinesthetic organization. That is, to produce a desired effect on something, we try to coordinate as efficiently as possible all the parts of our system necessary to our action. Whatever terms we use to describe the nonphysical aspects of our functioning also come into play in any of our actions. We can strengthen these nonphysical aspects by becoming more aware of them and of the part they play in our techniques. But martial artists who do not entertain these concepts and simply apply themselves wholeheartedly and singlemindedly to their endeavors are capable of the same focus of energy and generation of power as are those who speak constantly of *chi*.

Emphasis on *chi* is often accompanied by the idea that we need not use physical strength in our techniques. It is, however, mistaken to believe that an overall philosophy of giving way, or yielding to an opponent's attack, eschews strength. From a practical standpoint, after we have neutralized or deflected an opponent's attack, or even while we are engaged in neutralizing, we must counterattack with enough power to incapacitate him. We might accomplish this by a blow or kick, by a throw, or by a joint lock.

As I experience and observe what goes on in various forms of hand-to-hand fighting, I see clearly that strength of one sort or another plays an important part. Obviously, our legs have to be strong to provide stability and balance, and we must be able to generate enough physical power to disable an opponent when an opening presents itself. Even where strength is relegated to a minor role, as is true of tai chi, it comes into its own at certain moments. But it is also true that adherents of soft systems use strength in a different way from those who follow hard ones. The range of systems might be thought of as a continuum from very hard to very soft. Leaving such factors as speed and technique aside for the moment, at one extreme students practice to build muscular strength and physical bulk both as protection against attacks that might get through their defenses and as the basic ingredient of their own offensive and defensive techniques. At the other extreme the intention is to be almost ephemeral when attacked and to counterattack those areas that are exposed, or "empty," with a wavelike flow of power dependent only in part on muscular strength.

Although for purposes of discussion we can speak of systems as spread along this continuum, I have observed that the fully rounded fighters do not allow themselves to be limited by the dictates of a particular style or system. They may start out in a system labeled hard or soft, but as the years go by and their skill increases, they become accomplished in almost all the possible ways of attacking and defending. Their knowledge and experience then make what they do difficult to categorize as hard or soft, external or internal. Depending on their assessment of a situation, they may choose to do one of the following: evade an attack, smother it once it begins, stop it before it really gains momentum and power, or parry it with a hard block. Usually, they will perform any of these techniques with equal facility. Generally, they will be relaxed until the instant they focus their power onto the target. Their own attack or their counter will be powerful and delivered in a way that will make it difficult or impossible for the opponent to escape.

In the self-defense I teach, I stress the softness and yielding characteristic of tai chi. But in order to prepare for more practical situations, I also favor supplementary methods and the judicious use of strength in dealing with opponents. For example, if we use a throw to counter an opponent's attack, and such a technique can be devastingly effective, we may employ a degree of strength that passes beyond the bounds recommended in tai chi. Joint locking techniques, also very effective against opponents, will not work if we hold the opponent too loosely and he slips from our grasp.

Those who are purists with regard to martial arts systems may take issue with my failure to follow only one system. Perhaps because my background includes training in more than one martial art, I am less committed than I might be to unswerving adherence to one particular system. I'm not convinced that total commitment to one system is a truly flexible approach.

In any discussion of fighting we must also consider such attributes as stamina, physical toughness, and the desire to survive or win. These attributes are not particularly dependent on style. I have witnessed matches in which one person surpassed another in skill but was defeated because of a deficiency in one of these qualities.

I know that my students are not training to become strong fighters, nor is their training geared to such a goal. But for better or worse I have introduced them to the methods of attack and defense I have evolved over the years. I hope that through this practice they can gain a small measure of fighting skill, and at least form minds and bodies fairly knowledgeable about and capable of personal defense.

In addition to developing self-defense skills, this additional training enables students to come to terms with aspects of themselves they might seldom otherwise encounter. For example, they are sometimes pushed beyond the physical limits within which they imagine themselves bound. When this occurs, they realize that when they really want to or need to they can exceed their own expectations. If they are hurt but not incapaci-

106

tated, they are encouraged to bear the pain stoically and to try to continue. Such stoicism and the determination not to give up constitute an attempt to direct the mind's attention from the injury to the requirements of attack or defense. Through these means, students are enabled to find out more about themselves, about how their minds and bodies work, and about the control they can exercise over themselves. They gain the confidence that comes with knowing they can overcome their pain and fear, and that their determination can carry them beyond imagined limits.

Still another important benefit of this training is the help it affords students to learn to focus their attention on the moment. A fast punch or kick directed at one of our vital points usually elicits an instant response. Under these circumstances, our mind cannot easily entertain thoughts unconnected with the present moment without our suffering some unwanted damage.

Finally, we should keep in mind that a situation has deteriorated considerably by the time the people involved actually physically touch each other. I advocate the growth of awareness in my students, because the ability to sense danger is really a more important self-defense attribute than fighting prowess. If we can foresee early enough that the course we are on will lead to the possibility of injury or worse, we will try to take action to avoid a collision or, if it seems unavoidable, to prepare to survive it.

Students are encouraged to turn their outer awareness inward as well. It is in their interest to quietly watch the rise and fall of their thoughts, to try to notice the origin of their thoughts and feelings, and thus to try to understand their mental processes better.

As for the content of my tai chi instruction, I have put major emphasis on push-hands, because I have found this training the most useful of any I know in helping us to break our usual patterns of thinking. Here we attempt to use a method of attack and defense that seems to oppose, or to be different from, our habitual approach to doing something. For example, in our everyday lives, pushing a shopping cart or opening a window takes a certain degree of strength. If the cart is loaded or the window is stuck, we apply more strength until we are able to move them. The use of additional strength usually produces the desired result.

Beginners in push-hands attempt to employ this same method. When attacking and encountering resistance they push more strongly, and when defending they attempt to avoid being pushed by resisting. Both methods run counter to tai chi principle and, from a practical standpoint, play into a more skillful opponent's hands. That is, if the more skilled suddenly releases pressure, the unwarranted degree of strength employed by the beginner in either pushing (attacking) or resisting a push (defending) results in an overextension and a consequent loss of balance.

On a more advanced level, finding an opponent's center (the target of an attack) may prove difficult. Here we may encounter little resistance as the opponent evades or neutralizes our push. But in our effort to catch up with the evasive actions we may move too quickly or attempt to use too much strength. As in the previous case, we usually find we have overextended and have lost our balance.

Learning to attack or defend in an unaccustomed way can change the way our mind works. By performing actions that are at variance with our usual ones or using methods that seem unworkable in our everyday lives, we slowly become open to additional possibilities for relating to the world. During the first months, or perhaps even years, of applying this new method of dealing with an opponent, we usually fail in every attempt. One day we experience success, but it is merely an isolated instance and may be followed by additional hundreds of unsuccessful efforts before the next success occurs. Naturally, success is gratifying and we become eager for more. However, such expectations can interfere with training, because we may become too intent on results and get discouraged when it all seems to take too long. It is helpful if we can hold to the thought that it is the effect on our minds of the process we are undergoing that is of primary importance and not success at pushing or resisting an opponent. An extreme example of the impatience for tangible results is the tendency of strong or athletic persons to use their strength or physical ability, because through this they can achieve their mistaken surface objective of winning. But they will, then, be practicing in a way that will deny them far more important benefits.

As noted earlier, one of our aims is to attempt to break the hold of our conditioning on our minds. Our push-hands training will help us to do this. But such work is not altogether pleasant, because it usually entails giving up what is comfortable and trying to behave in a way that is different, and alien to our "normal" behavior.

The slowness with which results are achieved in tai chi for most students is really of great benefit to them, because through this they can learn to "let go." When the changes they expect from their form or push-hands practice are not apparent quickly enough, those who persist begin to give up their preconceptions of achieving some imagined end in tai chi. Again, through this they are helped to recognize that benefits lie in the process and not in reaching a goal. When they see they are capable of changing lifelong patterns of moving and reacting, they begin to open to the idea that they need not be limited to only one way of dealing with the world or that only one way of acting or doing something is right. These ideas, and generally learning to let go, are reinforced by our emphasis on releasing tension and relaxing.

Other nonphysical dimensions of the tai chi and self-defense I teach concern the chance for students to use confrontation, wherever or in whatever form it occurs, to learn more about themselves and others. For example, interactions with people whose interests oppose ours sometimes make us feel frustrated and angry. This could happen with an opponent in push-hands or sparring, or it could take place with someone outside the *dojo*. Of course, when we practice we are taught to keep our minds clear and unruffled by extraneous thoughts and feelings. If such thoughts claim our attention, we will lose our concentration and some of our effectiveness. We try to maintain a relatively restrained and detached state of mind outside the *dojo* as well, taking whatever action we sense is appropriate, even none at all, although we may be provoked by someone who seems to have taken unfair advantage of us or to have offended us in some way. After such an exchange, however, we might review the possible causes of a negative interaction, examining our minds on whatever levels are open to us for reasons for the confrontation and for the feelings we experienced. A number of insights could result from developing and using our inner awareness and looking at confrontation in this way.

To take one possible instance, suppose we get angry, become aware of the feeling, and later attempt to find its cause. Usually we discover that we become angry because people don't behave or act in ways we think fair, appropriate, or correct. On closer examination we may find that our assessment of people's behavior turns on basic conceptions or sets of beliefs about how the world is ordered. If we hold fixed and perhaps even strong ideas about right and wrong, and about how events should proceed, we are likely to become upset and disappointed when life goes contrary to our thinking. As we become aware that we hold definite views on how people should behave and the world should run, and that these views are in large part responsible for our feelings of anger and frustration, we might attempt to alter our views or reduce their strength. Such a change could come about, as our mind and our thinking mature, with the realization that our knowledge of the world and its workings is at best incomplete and imperfect. This understanding could lead us to reduce our estimate of the rightness of our ideas and make us more tolerant of other approaches and points of view. We might also begin to question both the goals we have set for ourselves and the degree of intensity, or perhaps ruthlessness and insensitivity toward others, with which we should strive toward them.

Because our cultural conditioning usually underlies our feelings about the right way for us and for others to behave, the training we do is designed to help us to break our conditioned patterns. Through greater self-understanding and an emphasis on the more intuitive part of the mind, which is thought to view life holistically, we attempt to achieve a more tranquil attitude and a broader outlook. Even where we continue to pursue the goals we think will make us happy, the suspicion that we are seeing a situation too narrowly or shallowly will begin to temper, and perhaps restrain, our pursuit. As training continues, a set of circumstances that may have threatened or upset us earlier will then lose some of its immediacy and power.

We all have a philosophy of life, a set of beliefs about how things work. Often these ideas have little to do with logic or reason, or they may have been useful in our childhood but not as useful as we matured. They may be the product of the effect of a powerful experience on us or of a basic nature that is strongly predisposed in a particular direction.

For example, let us suppose that we believe we must compete with and defeat others to get our share of the world's goods. As a consequence, we are likely to try to prepare our minds and bodies and to arrange our lives to enable us to deal successfully with anyone who wants what we want or who attempts to take what we have. If we think in this way we can easily support our view by evidence we see all around us that everyone is out for himself with little regard for most others. We will not notice or accept evidence that might support a contrary position.

Yet, we could just as easily put forward an opposing point of view and find the necessary evidence for it in our experience. This position would have it that life is essentially cooperative and that everything fits together to give us the world or universe we are a part of. This cooperation might be illustrated by individual cells joining one another to make our bodies, and atoms combining to form molecules and through whatever process building the physical world we know. It extends to our cooperating as individuals to form groups that we maintain both for survival and development. If we come to such a way of thinking about these processes, we would conduct our lives differently from people who fear a malevolent universe or must guard against being overcome by or losing out to others.

Some people have come to still another viewpoint concerning the most satisfying or least difficult way to live. They think it is makes sense to become less ambitious, to give up trying so hard to get something. "Something" could be material possessions, power, another person's love, or spiritual enlightenment. In this view, grasping after something creates misery and unhappiness. Another facet of this approach has it that life is change and that to attempt to stop change is to attempt the impossible. We suffer because of our desires and because we are unwilling to accept the changing flow of life and go with it.

The Taoists, for their part, would have us tamper as little as possible with the workings of the world. They advocate discovering the rhythm of life and then attempting to harmonize with it. In an oversimplified example of this viewpoint, it is natural to plant in the spring and to harvest in the fall. In general, to reverse this process would be totally unproductive. As we attempt to harmonize with the rhythms we discern in the world, the degree of effort given to an endeavor must be carefully calculated to avoid applying too much or too little.

In our search for answers we will come across the foregoing briefly mentioned theories and many others, and we may decide that one or some combination of them generally fits our world view. Our theory will have its learned proponents, who will present it in a fashion that accords with our culture's generally approved notions of reality and methods of determining it. I believe, however, that all theories of reality are flawed, because of the overwhelmingly great number of variables involved, capable of seemingly infinite interpretation, and perhaps more important, because of the mystery that ultimately underlies existence. Moreover, in my experience, embracing or relying on a particular theory is seldom enough to insulate us, if that is our intention, from the immediacy of physical, mental, or emotional suffering. It seems impossible for us to live in a way that will completely avoid physical and mental abrasions. Perhaps some degree of suffering is a consequence of being alive, and perhaps even full understanding of how the world works (if it were possible) is not proof against feeling pain.

A physical illustration of this point seems especially apt. If we stub a toe or hit a finger with a hammer, knowing consciously or subconsciously that we might have intended to hurt ourselves does little to remove the pain. Nor is pain eased by a knowledge of human physiology or an understanding of the processes involved in the registration in our minds of an injury to a toe or finger. It is true that we can train ourselves to focus our minds so that we can ignore pain, but it may not always be in our interest to do so. It could well be that pain and suffering has the function of getting our attention, clearing our sight, or helping us to a wiser way of life.

Reservations concerning the imperfections of human life and understanding do not mean we should forgo the attempt to make sense of things. Achieving even limited understanding, and following certain general directions, does help us to lessen the force of, or possibly avoid, many disasters and intellectual or emotional upsets.

In a kind of self-defense, we probably all try to discover a method that might make periodic abrasions easier to bear. I must state again, however, that I believe no method—or enlightenment, for that matter—is proof against life. That is, any system we might develop or come to for avoiding or substantially reducing the difficulties of life or the distress they cause is going to be imperfect—somehow unfinished—and will not explain or handle every eventuality. There seems always to be more for us to learn and to understand. It could well be that no matter what degree of understanding we have reached we will continue to set ourselves new problems to solve.

The foregoing reservations harmonize with the point of view that has developed from my years of martial arts training. Basic to this view is the avoidance of extremes (including the extreme of believing that we have the definitive answer to how life is best lived). Too much development in one direction or too great an emphasis on one aspect of life is unbalanced. This, sooner or later, brings about some sort of collapse or disaster that makes necessary a withdrawal, or additional development, in another direction. We may be justified in taking a longer-range view of our lives, as in the theory of reincarnation. Then we might believe we are afforded the opportunity to try out one extreme in one life and a less extreme variation on it or even its opposite in another. But I am not certain about the availability of other lives and about how that system operates. I feel more secure about working with the life I have and about doing the best I can with it.

If we accept this line of thinking, we will attempt to be careful to keep a middle way, a kind of moderation in whatever we do. Tai chi push-hands is excellent for helping us learn this method, because it demonstrates clearly that any overextension in terms of strength or position usually results in loss of balance, which could be equated with disaster. On the other hand, doing too little or doing less than is required also is unsatisfactory.

Timing is also an important element in responding appropriately to some challenge. We must be careful to respond neither too early nor too late to a situation that demands our attention. Both early and late constitute extremes of a sort and must be avoided if we wish to be successful.

To expand our discussion slightly, I believe that our natures are inclined in a particular direction. Eastern and Western astrological, numerological, and psychological systems attempt to delineate the nature and degree of this inclination. But despite possessing certain predilections, we need not be tied to only one way of responding to a situation. For example, some people believe that they are by nature shy and retiring and have no choice but to react in that way to every incident in their lives. Others believe they are strong and aggressive and must deal with problems by not backing down or by overpowering those who oppose them. But a set response or approach might be successful in one instance or even in a number of instances, only to suddenly fail because circumstances have altered.

Thus, it seems an inadequate or mistaken design to depend on only one way of handling situations. We should learn to avoid a fixed response, using instead a measure of strength or forceful action where it is appropriate and giving way where that seems of value. Nor is it only a question of choosing between the use or avoidance of force; it is also a matter of having at one's disposal a whole range of possible replies. An example is, obviously, the action of the mature and skillful martial artist who successfully meets an adversary's attack by seeming to choose one or more appropriate techniques from among a number he has perfected. Of course, such a person does not consciously assess the nature of an attack and then select a reply. The whole process happens too quickly to permit such a relatively slow reaction. Rather, because of his years of training, his mind and body work in a way that allows a spontaneous and almost instantaneous reaction to a stimulus, bypassing a conscious selection from among alternative possibilities.

At any rate, if we are by nature nonassertive, it would be advantageous to work to become somewhat more aggressive in pursuing or defending our interests. If we lean in the opposite direction, we may need to develop a softer and more yielding reaction to encounters. In addition, it is hoped that we will learn a greater variety of responses, or that we will gain in awareness and subtlety of action as we acquire experience.

An attempt to avoid extremes, and to apply only enough effort to attain our ends, requires very refined judgment. First of all, we have to decide what is worth doing. Then in the doing of it, we have to sense both when we are going beyond the bounds of moderation and when we are using too little energy to achieve results. We must be careful to act neither too early nor too late. This means also that in our endeavors we must determine how much application over time, or persistence, constitutes an appropriate degree of effort.

Neither is living our lives just a question of arranging things to minimize or avoid suffering. Many other considerations play a part. To reduce everything to just a pleasure-pain principle is mistaken. But let us say that to conduct our lives reasonably well, the few suggestions I have offered will be of help, and through continuous effort and application we might begin to make them part of ourselves. Our lives seem also to be lived, however, on levels other than the everyday one to which most of us are attuned. I sense that on other levels, which may have to do with the spirit, or whatever that aspect of ourselves is termed, we may *choose* illness, injury, difficult or ill-fated relationships, or other disasters because we wish to learn from them. As stated earlier, we may decide to experience circumstances that a sensible person would wish to avoid.

Such speculation gives us pause about making pronouncements concerning the best way to live. We all seem to be slightly different from one another, and these differences make for uniqueness in the way we conduct our lives. There may be no "correct" or "right" way to deal with a problem or to order the various threads of our lives.

Yet, although different ways of dealing with a particular problem are possible and although we may intentionally choose a course of action that leads to calamity, it is probably useful for us to remain awake. This attitude of mind entails trying to pay attention to what we think and do throughout the day. It should extend even to learning about and becoming conscious of our dream life. It rests on the premise that we are affected by everything we do and that each of our actions affects others and, for that matter, everything in the universe. To pay attention, we need a strong, flexible, and open mind. The mind here is not thought of in just its logical, analytical functioning but also in its intuitive role. All these qualities of mind can be developed and enhanced through training.

CHAPTER XII

Summary

"What I know of the divine sciences and Holy
Scripture, I learnt in woods and fields. I have had
no other masters than the beeches and the oaks."

ST. BERNARD

IT APPEARS THAT our understanding of life and our decisions about
how we should live it will not come from our having figured everything
out, because the whole picture is just too complex. We know very little
with certainty, especially if we confine "knowledge" to the use of our
rational faculties. Our intuitive grasp of reality also does not grant us
anywhere near the degree of certainty we might desire.

What is it, then, that makes each of us choose our unique way of living?
If we live in a modern-day developed nation, the communications media
will ensure that we encounter any number of philosophic viewpoints. Why
do we select one over another? In addition to the rather important pull
of our basic inclination, I think our choice of a way to live depends largely
on the degree of our mental and spiritual development. As we begin to
see more clearly or increase our awareness, our choices in life will usually
reflect these changes. I believe that certain training methods pursued over
a period of years help encourage and promote this development.

In my experience, the Asian martial arts, engaged in as meditative
training, can promote our unfolding by grounding us and giving us a
general sense of becoming more settled, centered, or tranquil. The practices
of learning to move from and concentrating on our lower abdominal area
(the *tan tien* or *tanden*), to be fully in each moment, to examine and let go
of preconceived ideas, and to relax physically and mentally all seem to

prepare us to open up to seeing the world more clearly. The ideas that then seem to appear in our conscious minds, or which begin to seem right, have to do with our recognition of our connectedness with other people and with the earth, and of the unity and interrelatedness of all that exists. This development does not proceed merely in a material sense but is accompanied by a rise in our appreciation of the spirit that permeates everything. Such an appreciation brings with it the kind of regard and respect for what is around us that, at its best or most developed, goes beyond a subject-object view of the world to one that sees that there is really no separation between everything that exists. Recognizing the manner in which things are connected and ordered causes us to try to discern and then to harmonize with the rhythm of life.

These realizations do not come from an immersion in some other culture, although such contact can help us break the hold our own conditioning has on our thinking. Nor do they come from attempting to follow in our daily lives the outer trappings of another culture.

All of the foregoing benefits or results of training seem to come about gradually. Of course, viewed in another way the changes occur suddenly and seemingly spontaneously as we come to insights or see connections that previously were obscure. But though these insights come instantaneously, training seems to prepare the field for their emergence and they are more likely to appear when we prepare ourselves in this way than when we do not.

Some will not be content with the benefits of martial arts training I have mentioned nor with the gaining of periodic insights, and they will want nothing less than full spiritual awakening. Their main reason for training is their hope, or expectation, that sooner or later they will reach this goal. They may even forsake secular life and immerse themselves fully for varying lengths of time, or for all of their lives, in training designed to bring them enlightenment. Unfortunately, there is no guarantee that they will achieve a full awakening even if they practice diligently, lead an exemplary life (by whatever standards), or are taught by a fully liberated teacher. As with just about everything else that comes to us in life, our awakening should probably be considered a gift that may or may not be given us. It is not something we can buy or get by working hard or behaving in some approved way.

Nevertheless, the bestowal of this gift seems more likely if we live our lives in a way that spiritual masters have from ancient times thought conducive to our awakening. The rightness or correctness for us of this path or way of living becomes increasingly evident as our clarity of mind and our understanding develop. It sometimes seems that we have limited choice in these matters. Our particular stage of development usually leads us to do what we do. We are almost always in our rightful place in life and are given the understanding and vision we are able to handle. Change is a constant factor in all of life. We change what we do, or are changed, when we are ready. Thus, those who are prepared to embark on the training I advocate will be drawn to it.

Probably only very few of us will achieve full spiritual awakening in our lifetime no matter what we do. But we may wish to lead our lives in the belief that such a development is possible and that it will come when we are ready for it. Training in a discipline that can help to prepare us for a breakthrough will strongly attract some of us. The benefits that accrue along this path, in terms of improved physical and mental health and well-being, and enhanced understanding and insight (limited though it may be), are quite valuable in themselves. Moreover, we have not closed the door to further development but rather have left it open for an ultimate breakthrough.